To: Doris + Danny 6/1/74
With all best wishes
Gene Miller

YOUR FUTURE IN SECURITIES

YOUR FUTURE IN SECURITIES

By
EUGENE MILLER

RICHARDS ROSEN PRESS, INC.
New York, New York 10010

Standard Book Number: 8239–0291–9
Library of Congress Catalog Card Number: 73–86318
Dewey Decimal Classification: 371.42

Published in 1974 by Richards Rosen Press, Inc.
29 East 21st Street, New York City, N.Y. 10010

First Edition

Manufactured in the United States of America

About the Author

EUGENE MILLER is a leading financial executive with long experience and keen interest in the securities field. He served for five years at the New York Stock Exchange, becoming Senior Vice-President of marketing and investor services. Previously he was Vice-President of McGraw-Hill, Inc., Associate Managing Editor of *Business Week,* and City Editor of the Greensboro (North Carolina) *Daily News*. In 1973 he moved to a new post as Senior Vice-President of CNA Financial Corporation.

Born in Chicago, Illinois, he received a B.S. degree in chemical engineering from the Georgia Institute of Technology; an A.B., magna cum laude, from Bethany College; an M.S. from the Graduate School of Journalism of Columbia University; and an M.B.A. from the Graduate School of Business Administration of New York University. He also holds a diploma for graduate work at Oxford University, England, and an LL.D. degree from Bethany College. During World War II he served aboard a destroyer. He is currently a Commander in the United States Naval Reserve.

Mr. Miller is a frequent author and lecturer on financial

topics. He is Adjunct Professor of Finance at the Graduate School of Business of Fordham University and a Trustee of Bethany College. His professional affiliations include membership in the National Association of Business Economists, the American Economics Association, the Society of American Business Writers, and the American Finance Association.

Mr. Miller is married and the father of three children.

Contents

Introduction

Sometimes the last line of a book can serve as well as its first line.

"Today, your future in securities offers you opportunities to participate and contribute in ways that your predecessors—those who made this book for you—were seldom able to dream of."

Opportunities spring from change. And few industries are as reflective of our society's massive process of change today as the securities industry. No time in the nearly two hundred years of America's financial marketplaces has been so rapid and important a succession of responses to the growing and altering needs of the society that this industry serves. This is true not only of business needs, but also of the needs of the society as a whole—the role that a viable and responsive securities industry can and must play in serving the total life-style of its day.

Change is just one of the themes of this book. Another theme is found at the book's start and continues as a thread throughout its pages. It is the discussion: What the industry really does . . . its primary and crucial role in the capital formation process that provides the financial fuel for all of the society's institutions, public and private. This process is nothing less than the creation of money, in the sense of identifying sources of funds and bringing them to areas in need of funds—whether these are businesses, governments, or any of the agencies that bridge the gap between the two.

A final theme is the increasingly worldwide identity of the securities industry. America's financial structures had their clear antecedents in the same European trade developments that brought the modern world, including America itself, into being. Today, all of the world's mature capital markets, and those of developing areas all around the globe, are coming to work in concert as never before in mankind's history. Thus, a career in securities today, by the same definition that is beginning to rule careers of every sort, is an intentional career.

Change . . . the capital formation process . . . the multinationalization of our world. As you consider a career in securities, these three themes will form the intertwined framework against which you consider your decisions and goals. The three are inseparable—for proof of this, only read this morning's newspaper or a copy of any current magazine. If this changing world of finance interests you as a place to work, this book will help to set the scene for you. At the New York Stock Exchange, and throughout the industry, we deal with the financial challenges of our times on a daily basis. We welcome your interest in our industry, and we would welcome your participation in our efforts to meet its challenges.

James J. Needham
Chairman
New York Stock Exchange

YOUR FUTURE IN SECURITIES

CHAPTER I

What the Industry Really Does

The story is told of two characters who were flying over the ocean for the first time. "Wow!" said one. "Look at all that water down there." "Yeah," said the other. "And that's only the top!"

If you have picked up this book, it is reasonable to suppose that there is something about a career in the securities industry that interests you. Whether or not that is so, there are some less well-known facts about the securities field, and the role it plays in our society, that give this career area a high rating when it comes to seeking and selecting a job. The industry is an unusually interesting place to work. There is a great variety of jobs to choose from. The work is both economically and socially useful. And the financial rewards can be great.

As it happens, you are looking at one of the broadest and most far-reaching career fields of the coming decades. Like the ocean whose dimensions fascinated our flying friends, the scope of the securities field is hard to grasp all at once. This has been increasingly true as the industry has developed, especially in recent years. And changes taking place right now are going to mean a greatly expanded role for the industry in the future—one that will dwarf even its very substantial achievements to date.

When we say "securities," of course, most of us think first of the stockbroker who buys and sells shares in companies for investors. We know something about his job and the office where he works, and about some of the other jobs that probably go with such an office. But the stockbroker and his office are just one very visible part of a financial services industry that has an immense job to do today and will have an even larger and more important job to do from now on.

That job is one of "capital formation." The securities industry has a central part in raising, and in a real sense *creating,* the funds that fuel large parts of the American economy—and other economies around the world—as they expand and grow both to do business and to serve the nonbusiness needs of their people. The industry is the middleman in the capital formation process. It brings together people who need money with people who have money to invest.

Some of the economic numbers that go with this job are impressive, if not staggering. We in the United States are now living in a trillion-dollar economy. The total U.S. Gross National Product, which is the value of all the goods we make and sell to each other plus the services we provide for each other, reached this unimaginable level in 1971. At current growth rates, compounded for the rest of the decade, the Gross National Product will have reached—or exceeded—*two* trillion dollars by 1980.

The capital dollars needed for growth within this national economic framework are on the same impressive scale. It was estimated in 1970 that the economy would need nearly half a trillion dollars to support its projected growth by 1975. Our corporations would need nearly $200,000,000,000 to finance their long-range operations and plans. A similar sum would be needed for home mortgages. Our cities would need nearly $100,000,000,-000 to fund their physical growth and services. And capital needs at even higher levels are expected in the last five years of the 1970's. In particular, governments at every level—local, state, and federal—are sharply increasing their demands on the capital supply. One economist has said that *half* of all demands on the capital markets will soon come, not from business organizations, but from the so-called public sector—our governments and the services they make available to us as citizens.

The securities industry is at the very center of the capital markets. The banking system, certainly, is an important source of lending power for capital needs. But it is the securities industry that provides the marketplaces where money for both business and public use is generated in a broad range of forms and by a broad array of methods. The great and growing demand on these marketplaces, where the demand for money always seems to outrun the supply, is leading now to more and more innovation in creating and using capital. And this, in turn, is leading to a greater number and variety of interesting jobs at every level of the securities field.

The stockbroker and the shares of stock he buys and

sells for his investor-customers are a major part of one important way in which a company raises the money it needs to operate and expand. Today, according to the latest survey of the New York Stock Exchange, nearly 32,000,000 people—almost a sixth of the U.S. population—are individual shareowners or stockholders. Twice that many—bringing the total to half of the population—are shareowners in an indirect way, through their participation in mutual funds, investment clubs, pension funds, profit-sharing plans, and other "pooled" or "institutional" shareholding organizations. Individual shareowners are projected to reach 50,000,000 by 1980, and institutional share ownership is expected to grow at least proportionately.

Some 30,000 American companies have sold their shares to the public. There are perhaps 25,000,000,000 shares of stock owned by investors today—with a market value in mid-1973 of $1.2 trillion. But then remember that this investment process has taken place over a period of nearly two hundred years—and that the securities industry will help companies sell stock worth at least another $400,000,000,000 just by the end of this decade. You are now glimpsing just one portion of the new and vastly greater capital formation process in which the industry will play a leading part.

Shares of stock come in two basic forms—common and preferred—and there are also variations such as preferred stock that is later convertible to common stock. But stock is only one method that a company uses to raise money in the financial marketplaces maintained by the securities industry. There are also many forms of corporate bonds, the total of which were worth more than $250,000,000,000 in the marketplace in 1973. These, too, are sold to investors on behalf of corporations by the firms in the securities business.

Nor, as we have seen, are corporations by any means the only seekers of capital in the financial markets. Governments at every level from the United States itself down to cities and small towns finance their services by issuing securities, usually bonds, and this is one of the fastest growing portions of the financial world. United States government securities outstanding in mid-1973 totaled nearly $500,000,000,000. State and local governments and their agencies accounted for another $200,000,000,000 in securities held by investors of all kinds—individuals, corporations, and financial institutions. Again, securities firms play a major part in the issuing and placing of all the different forms of government issues.

Many people, in fact, do not fully understand the social value of the securities industry's work with governments and the other areas that make up the public sector. Governments, we all know, are heavily supported by the taxes we pay. But taxes can only be stretched so far, and governments have come to rely in important ways on the capital markets to raise the funds they need. This reliance is growing as a percentage each year. And this situation is just as true of other "public" institutions—schools and colleges, hospitals and other health care centers, and local utilities and services.

The cost of money is an all-important factor, not only in private business, but also in the expansion of government services and the creation of new ones. Expanding a school system or a hospital facility—or building a new one—depends often on the cost of the funds to finance such projects. At the same time, attracting investors' money to these projects depends on paying an adequate return for the use of that money—or providing tax advantages and other incentives to make the investment worthwhile for various kinds of investors. The securities industry acts as the agent in working out agreeable terms between the public sector and the private sources of capital. And it is playing an increasingly creative role in devising bond issues and other forms of investment that satisfy the needs of both sides of the marketplace.

These same social purposes are often served in the opposite direction—bringing together the interests of business enterprises and government authorities to devise ways that business can meet its social responsibilities at a lower cost. Financing of pollution control is one example. Securities firms in recent years have been responsible for developing and selling various kinds of pollution-control revenue bonds to finance cleaner oil refineries and utility plants located in municipal industrial districts. The same techniques have been used to finance pollution-free plants built by community-owned utilities.

Urban redevelopment projects have also been the beneficiary of the expanded spirit of partnership between government, business, and the financial community. Entire sections of cities have been rebuilt by business interests using capital raised through the sale of securities. Entire new towns have been financed and built in the same way. So have major new airports, shipping ports, and mass-transportation systems.

The list could go on and on. These examples give a measure of the activity that takes place in an economy like that of the United States, and of the scope of its capital needs—needs that always seem to outdistance the amounts of money available to meet them. The role of the securities industry, and the primary economic function it performs, is to raise that capital and to try to close the challenging gap between the supply of money and the demand for it.

One more point to remember, as we begin to look at the securities industry as a place to work, is that this role is by no means limited to serving American interests. As large as the U.S. economy is, it is only one of a great many large and small economies around the world. The interrelationships between the U.S. financial system and those of other countries and economic blocs are already extensive, and the economies of the world are growing more closely related all the time.

Similarly, the securities industry is more and more an international business. Opportunities are by no means confined to the United States or to any other one country. In fact, it is certain that tomorrow's securities employee will be every bit as much of an internationalist—or "multinationalist"—as his or her counterpart anywhere else in the global village of our worldwide society.

CHAPTER II

A Brief Look at History

We talk today of the "global village" and "multinational business" as though these were new ideas. Really, of course, they are new words for ideas that are centuries old in the affairs of mankind. These concepts predate by hundreds of years even our modern system of nation-states. Their origins, in fact, go back to the first commercial trade that developed between different parts of the world. Trade goals led to the discovery of most of the rest of the world by the early European explorers, and to the growth of trading relationships between nations and continents by the mercantilists of the sixteenth and seventeenth centuries.

Today's modern securities industry grew from the same seeds that spawned our overall business system at least five centuries ago. The securities firms we see now had their earlier counterparts in the British and continental European merchant banking firms that were founded early in the eighteenth century—the Rothschilds in Germany, the Barings even earlier in Germany and England, the Hambros in Denmark and England. The financial techniques that we call "investment banking" in the United States still go under the name of "merchant banking" in The City—London's financial district that is the counterpart to our Wall Street. Lehman Brothers, Inc., one of our best-known American investment banking firms, was founded in New York in 1850 by Henry Lehman, the immigrant son of a cattle merchant in Würzburg, Germany. Many of the other long-established and prestigious firms in the securities industry also had their commercial origins in European families.

"Wall Street" is constantly used as a synonym for the securities industry. And that street is the actual center of the leading financial district in the United States—a picturesque and fascinating area of a few square blocks on the lower end of Manhattan Island in New York City that can rightly claim to be *the* financial capital of the country and of the world. Other major cities have their main financial streets as well—LaSalle Street in Chicago, Spring Street in Los Angeles, Montgomery Street in San Francisco.

But Wall Street was the actual site, in 1792, of the founding of the American securities industry—and, simultaneously, of what would become its leading marketplace, the New York Stock Exchange. Wall Street was the first political capital of the new nation, too, and the scene of many key events in the formation of the United States. There, as early as 1768—several years before the American Revolution—the organization later known as the New York State Chamber of Commerce campaigned against the notorious Stamp Act of the British Parliament and its taxes on the sale of tea in the colonies. George Washington took his first oath of office as President in Wall Street. The new government was organized there. The first U.S. Congress met there, and the Bill of Rights was adopted there.

Significantly, for the future securities industry, the first U.S. government stock was issued in Wall Street—an $80,000,000 issue authorized by the new Congress in 1789 to help pay the costs of the war that had just ended. Oher stocks were appearing, too, as the first "American" businessmen formed banks and insurance companies to handle the nation's first business. Alexander Hamilton himself helped to found the First United States Bank, and he was also a founder of some of the earliest American manufacturing companies, in New Jersey.

At first, though, these were stocks without a stock market. Trading in these first securities took place on a chance basis in coffeehouses, auction rooms, and offices in the Wall Street area. But the trading was sporadic and disorganized, and so it was hard to attract buyers—investors—because they could not be confident that they would be able to sell their securities whenever they wanted to.

The New York Stock Exchange was born literally under a tree. On May 17, 1792, a group of twenty-four merchants and auctioneers signed an agreement to meet daily under a buttonwood tree on Wall Street, and to be available there to accept the public's buy and sell orders. The first securities traded were the government's stock, the shares of the new insurance companies, and shares in the new banks—Hamilton's First United States Bank; the Bank of North America, which had been founded in

The New York Stock Exchange had its origin on May 17, 1792, under a buttonwood tree on Wall Street in New York City.

Philadelphia in 1784; and the Bank of New York, also founded in 1784 in the Wall Street area.

In a year, the new stock exchange was able to move indoors. Its members now met in the Tontine Coffee House that had just been built at the corner of Wall Street and William Street. This was a block from the site of the present New York Stock Exchange—where, in those years, stood Alexander Hamilton's house. Soon after 1800, the exchange moved to a meeting room at nearby 40 Wall Street, but it did not arrive at its present location on Broad Street near Wall Street until 1863.

Trading on the new exchange expanded as the nation's business, commercial, and transportation systems grew. After the War of 1812, the state of New York issued bonds to finance the Erie Canal, and these were traded in Wall Street. In 1817, the exchange adopted its first constitution, formally creating the "New York Stock Exchange Board." This established trading procedures and a means of setting commissions on trading activity. The names of stocks on the exchange were called out at 11:30 each morning, and the brokers made their bids to buy and offers to sell.

By 1827, the stocks of twelve banks and nineteen marine and fire insurance companies were traded on the exchange. So was the stock of the Delaware & Hudson Canal Company. The first American public utility—the New York Gas Light Company—brought its stock to the exchange. And in the 1830's, a new transportation security—stocks in the first railroads—were added to the list. Manufacturing companies were forming and growing rapidly now and found their investors through the New York marketplace.

In 1863, as the exchange moved to its present location, it adopted its modern name—New York Stock Exchange. In 1868, for the first time, existing memberships could be sold to new members. In 1871, the early trading process of calling out the names of the listed stocks was changed to continuous day-long trading. In 1879, the first "specialist" firms were established to maintain orderly trading in stocks, and the first telephones were used in exchange transactions. Trading first reached a daily volume of 1,000,000 shares in 1886; by the late 1960's,

A view of the present New York Stock Exchange building, at Broad and Wall streets.

daily trading would reach levels in the tens of millions of shares, and would hit a record of more than 31,700,000 shares in one day on August 16, 1971, in response to President Richard M. Nixon's announcement of new economic policies.

Modernization has come rapidly to the securities industry and its marketplaces in recent years. Computers and data processing methods have been brought to bear on the rapid rise of trading volume and the resulting need for more timely and sophisticated records. Trading transactions were first linked to the New York Stock Exchange's own computer system in 1965. A central depository for securities certificates was established in 1970 to help reduce the need for physical transfer of the increased numbers of shares being traded. Stock certificates, as well as bonds, can now be processed by means of standardized, machine-readable identification numbers. Individual firms, as well as the exchanges, have upgraded their information-handling technology. More and more, the business of the securities industry is being performed and recorded electronically and utilizing the services of vast arrays of computers.

There also have been human responses to the growing complexities of the securities industry. The New York Stock Exchange had been reorganized in 1938, following the stock-market "crash" of 1929 and the Depression of the 1930's; and the exchange was headed for the first time by a salaried president—William McChesney Martin, who later became chairman of the board of governors of the United States Federal Reserve System. In 1972, the job of president of the exchange was changed to chairman, and the first paid chairman chosen by the board was James J. Needham, who had been a member of the industry's chief regulatory agency, the Securities and Exchange Commission. The board itself was restructured to include ten members representing public interests as well as ten members from the securities industry itself. One of the new public members was the exchange's first woman director, Dr. Juanita M. Kreps, professor of economics at Duke University.

This is just an outline of the course the securities industry has followed since its first twenty-four representatives met under the Wall Street buttonwood tree more than 180 years ago. But for all its modest beginnings, the marketplace they founded then grew steadily and logically into the largest and most effective creator of business and government capital that exists anywhere in the world today.

CHAPTER III

An Outline of the Securities Industry

We have seen enough now of the nationwide and worldwide role of the securities field to realize that our stockbroker and his office are just one part—"only the top"—of a very large industry. Now, let us look at some of the dimensions of the industry itself, where it is located, and how it is organized.

Many of our key industries are large, highly concentrated into a few companies, and employ millions of people—many of them in relatively unspecialized jobs. Good examples of this are the automobile manufacturers, the steelmakers, and the energy and chemical industries.

The securities industry, by contrast, employs nearly a quarter of a million people whose jobs are both varied and considerably more specialized. The industry is also quite "fragmented"—its employees work for thousands of different firms throughout the country and the world, as well as for the exchanges on which the bulk of their business is done.

In 1972, there were nearly 5,000 brokerage firms registered with the Securities and Exchange Commission. Nearly 600 of these brokers, including most of the larg-

A typical scene in the Bond Room of the New York Stock Exchange.

An active day on the trading floor of the New York Stock Exchange.

est, are member firms of the New York Stock Exchange. About 150,000 people work for what is called the Exchange Community—all of the member firms as well as the exchange, which itself is a corporation and employs about 3,000 people.

Officers and partners of the member firms of the New York Stock Exchange account for about 6,000 jobs. There are some 52,000 registered representatives—securities sales people—and some 94,000 personnel in other jobs. Then, there are an estimated 70,000 additional people who work elsewhere in the industry—for firms that hold memberships on various smaller and regional exchanges around the country, or for firms that deal in the "over-the-counter" market, shares that are not listed on stock exchanges.

The New York Stock Exchange is the senior U.S. securities marketplace. Not only does the Exchange Community employ about three fourths of the people who work in the securities industry, but the exchange itself accounts for about the same percentage of dollar volume and numbers of shares sold on *all* registered exchanges. That business has grown dramatically in the past forty years. In 1935, the level of business transacted on the New York Stock Exchange was $13,300,000,000. By 1972, that business had grown more than twelve times—to $160,000,000,000. Trading volume that had run 1,000,000 shares a day in 1935 was running 16,000,000 shares in 1972. The New York Stock Exchange accounted for 80 percent of all the shares sold on stock exchanges.

The American Stock Exchange, which is also in New York and is a marketplace for generally smaller and less mature companies, accounted for another 10 percent. The remaining 10 percent was done on smaller exchanges—the National Stock Exchange, which trades stocks in New York for a number of small companies, and the regional exchanges, the major ones being the Boston Stock Exchange, the Midwest Stock Exchange in Chicago, the Pacific Stock Exchange located in both San Francisco and Los Angeles, the P-B-W Exchange in Philadelphia, and the Detroit Stock Exchange.

The over-the-counter business is made up of thousands of smaller firms that deal in securities not listed on the major or regional stock exchanges. There are perhaps 25,000 companies whose stocks (unlisted securities) are traded over the counter. While most of them are comparatively small, some of the nation's largest banks, insurance companies, and other financial institutions are traded in the over-the-counter market. The firms that trade in these stocks are all members of the National Association of Securities Dealers. They range from the largest brokers who deal in both listed and unlisted securities to the smallest firms that employ only a few people.

We see, then, that the securities business is quite widespread, both in the numbers and sizes of companies that make up the industry and in their geographical location. Where are securities firms located? New York, of course, is the major financial center, with three stock exchanges, many of the largest banks, and other concentrations of domestic business activity as well as many close links with business abroad. Thus New York, naturally enough, has a large number of securities companies. Of the 5,000 broker-dealers registered with the Securities and Exchange Commission, 1,096—more than 20 percent—are in New York City, and another 426 are located else-

The trading room at a large brokerage house.

where in the state of New York. California is the next state in order, with 525 registered firms. Then come New Jersey with 248, Pennsylvania with 239, Massachusetts with 200, Texas with 192, Illinois with 181, Florida with 136, and Ohio with 112. At the lower end of the scale are

Idaho with nine securities companies, West Virginia with eight, Nevada with seven, Alaska and Vermont with six, New Mexico with four, and South Dakota with three.

But the securities business is found wherever business of any kind is done—or wherever investors are located. A great many firms of substantial size are located in regional business centers and communities around the United States. The fifth largest brokerage firm in the industry, Dean Witter & Co., Inc., is headquartered in San Francisco and does business all around the country and overseas. Dain, Kalman & Quail, Inc., in Minneapolis; Prescott, Merrill, Turben, Inc., in Cleveland; and Wheat, First Securities, Inc., in Richmond are all important and successful securities firms in their regions of the country. Other leading regional firms are Boettcher & Company, in Denver; Howard, Weil, Labouisse, Friedrichs, Inc., in New Orleans; J. C. Bradford & Co., in Nashville; Robinson-Humphrey Company, Inc., in Atlanta; and Piper, Jaffray & Hopwood, Inc., in Minneapolis.

That helps to answer a question. Are the best opportunities for a person seeking a career in securities to be found in "Wall Street"? It is not an easy question. There is no doubt that Wall Street and New York are the focal point of the industry, just as Detroit is considered the center of the automobile business, and Pittsburgh leads among steel companies. Most of the largest and best-known securities firms in the business have their headquarters within a few blocks of each other in lower Manhattan, and the exchanges there are their primary marketplace.

But most of these firms also do important business elsewhere in the United States. As we have said, every city of reasonable size has important regional brokers headquartered there. And working away from New York can have many advantages. New York is a strongly competitive financial community, and it could be a good idea, at least at the start of your career, to work in a less competitive environment. Regional firms, and the local offices of national firms, may offer less pressure, more personal contact with customers, and a chance to try your hand at a variety of job experiences before you select the specialty that most interests you. Not all roads in the securities business—or any other business—lead to New York. But the opportunities on Wall Street itself are ample enough that the person who wants to work there can usually find a way when the time comes.

The stock exchanges themselves offer job possibilities that are interesting both as careers and as a broad introduction to the industry. A stock exchange serves several key purposes. It provides a marketplace for the trading activities of its members. It plays a coordinating role in the services that brokers provide for the investing public. It also provides important services to the members themselves in the form of statistics, research and economic analysis, and depositories for stock certificates and other financial documents. And, it serves a regulatory and surveillance role over the activities of the members, as well as representing them in their relations with government agencies, the Congress, and other financial marketplaces.

The jobs available at the stock exchanges, then, cover

a wide range of interests and disciplines. There are opportunities for people trained in accounting, law, economics, statistics, and public relations. Others have jobs helping companies meet the listing requirements of the exchange when they decide to have their shares listed and traded on that exchange. There are examiners and compliance managers who see to it that member firms meet the rules of the exchange. And there are several kinds of jobs on the trading floors of the exchanges—supervisors, clerks, messengers, and reporters who help keep the marketplace operating smoothly and assist in keeping records on trading activity. Finally, as computers and information processing equipment play a greater role in automating and recording securities transactions, there are jobs for data processing managers and computer programmers and technicians.

The New York Stock Exchange, as the largest marketplace, employs about 3,000 people in all of these activities. Employment at the American Stock Exchange is roughly 800 people. The smaller stock exchanges each have staffs of several hundred. A job at any of the major or regional exchanges can be a useful and productive career in itself—and also an effective way to gain a well-rounded idea of how the industry operates.

Nor should we overlook the Securities and Exchange Commission as a source of jobs. As the chief U.S. government agency concerned with the affairs of the securities industry, the SEC shares its regulatory role with the stock exchanges, and also shares with them the liaison role with Congress when any legislation affecting the industry is considered. In recent years, as the securities industry has grown larger and more complex in its operations, the SEC staff has expanded, and now represents some 1,500 jobs. Opportunities there are comparable in many ways to those at the New York Stock Exchange, with an emphasis on financial and legal training. Again, jobs at the SEC have provided many people interested in securities careers with a valuable overview of how the securities business works.

CHAPTER IV

Many Companies, Many Roles

By now you have an idea of how the securities industry fits into our economy, of its geography and marketplaces, and of its organizational outlines. Now we shall look at where by far the largest numbers of jobs are—in the 5,000 or so securities companies themselves.

Any industry with this many individual firms is bound to present a variety of activities and specialties that can be puzzling to the first-time observer. Remember, though, that there is a common theme. All of this activity takes place to accomplish one primary purpose: the generation of capital funds for our economy.

We can, in fact, compare the securities industry to a large company that manufactures a specific product for a particular market. General Motors, for example, makes vehicles for the transportation market. The securities industry's "product" is money—and its market is all the organizations, private and public, in the economy that use money.

Making a product, however—whether dollars or Ford Mustangs—is just one step in a long and logical sequence of steps. The process begins with planning: an analysis of the market's needs, and what products might

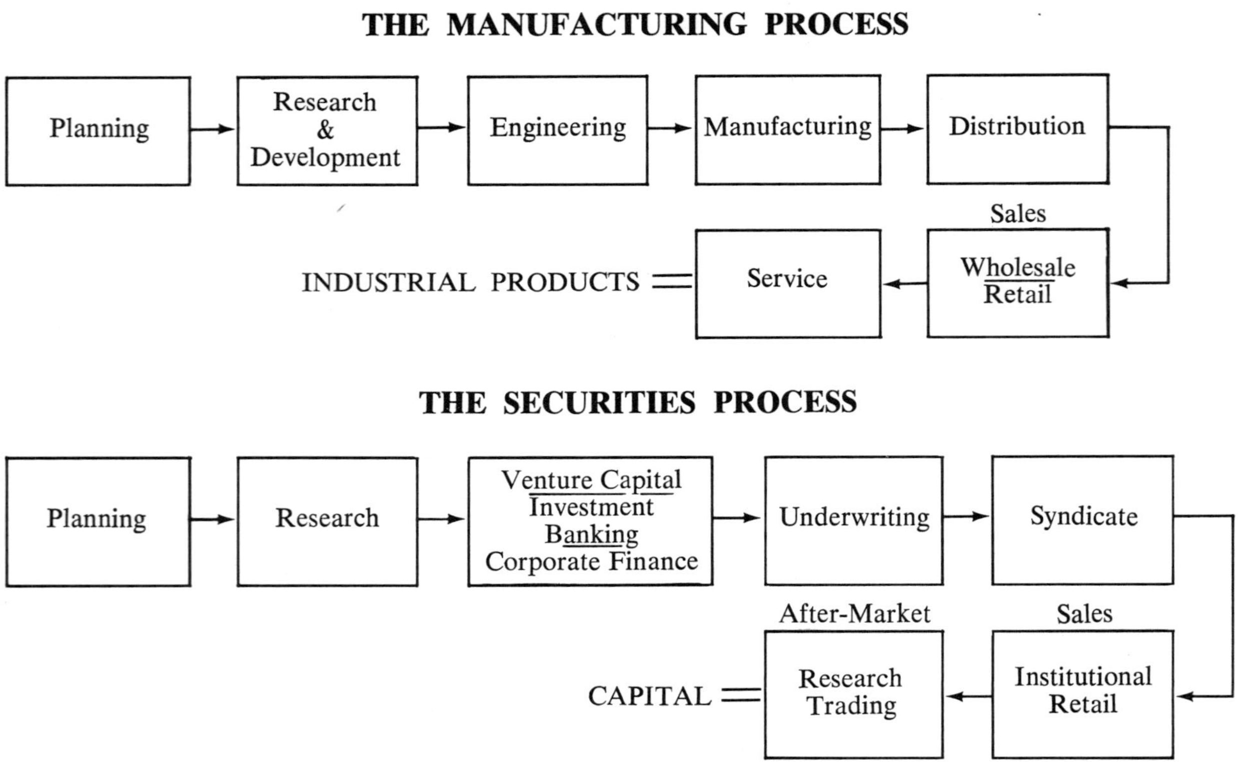

Chart comparing the manufacturing process and the securities process.

best serve those needs. Next comes research and development: what new resources and techniques can be applied to the market, and how can they be used in devising new products and improving products that already exist. A company's engineering department then gets down to the design of the product, and perhaps also the machinery to produce it. And now, after all of these earlier steps, the product is actually manufactured.

Even the manufacturing step occurs at a midpoint in the total process. Then the product must be distributed to the marketplace and sold to customers. Nearly all products, after they are sold and in the hands of the customers, must be serviced—not only to keep them in good repair, but also to keep the customer pleased and in a mood to come back to the same company for future purchases.

The process is not really so different for the securities industry from that for makers of automobiles and television sets. The "products" of the securities industry are not just stocks and bonds. They are all of the ways in which the industry serves the financial needs of its customers, whether they are corporations or governments or individual investors. In fact, it can be argued that such items as stocks and bonds are not the product at all. Rather, they are examples, among many others, of the *ways* themselves that the securities industry goes about generating capital. They are examples of devices, or techniques, that aid the work of finance. As such, they are a means to an end—not the end in itself.

Planning in a securities firm, as it is in any company,

is ultimately the responsibility of the top management. The firm's senior executives continually watch their customers' capital needs and uses of capital. They try to anticipate the trends in business and government, and the investment preferences of individuals, to learn what new investment products and services may be needed or welcomed. The important new area of pollution-control financing grew from just such an observed need of both corporations and governments for capital to meet environmental responsibilities. In the same way, investment pools such as mutual funds were developed to meet investors' desires to hold broad investments under conditions of less risk and without having to perform for themselves the tasks of individual evaluation of each security.

Research in a securities firm, in fact, performs this evaluation function on a broad basis. Its role is a continual review of all the securities traded in the marketplace to determine their merits for various kinds of investors and investment purposes. Securities research analysts must consider not only the companies whose securities are under consideration, but also the industries of which they are a part and the economic and business conditions in which they operate. Demands for products and services constantly shift, and so does the investment attractiveness of the stocks of the companies in each field.

Engineering and manufacturing, as practiced by securities firms, are the heart of the capital formation process and serve both sides of the securities marketplace—the investor of capital and the user of capital. A company raises money to fund its operations and expansion by selling stock that represents ownership in the company, or by issuing bonds that represent a form of borrowed debt. The securities firm helps to design and structure these issues, and then it finds investors to buy them. In the securities industry, this is called investment banking, or corporate finance, and the issuing of securities is called underwriting.

Another form of investment banking or corporate finance is the securing of "venture capital" for new companies whose stock is not yet acceptable in the public marketplace. Often venture capital is money raised from private investment sources, including securities firms themselves. And it is often provided to a new company in exchange for an interest in stock that may one day be underwritten as a public issue.

Distribution of securities is carried out by a process called syndication. The securities firm that designs the issue is the managing underwriter, and often several firms will join together in managing an issue. But even the largest firms can seldom sell an entire issue themselves, and so they gather a syndicate of other firms who each agree to take a portion of the securities to sell to their particular customers. Once the syndicate is assembled, a price is put on the individual shares, if it is a stock issue, that includes the amount that the company whose stock is being issued will get for each share, plus a percentage that is the underwriter's fee for handling the issue.

Sales and marketing in the securities industry is the largest single job area, because it is the area of greatest contact with the investing public. Securities and the other financial products of the industry are sold in a variety of ways. Again, the analogy of product marketing in any industry is useful. Many industrial products are sold at retail—directly to the final customer. Others are sold to wholesalers, who in turn sell to the retail customer. The same is true in the securities business.

We talked earlier of the 32,000,000 individual shareholders in the United States. These are the securities industry's retail customers—those for whom the stockbroker, or registered representative, trades and manages investment accounts on a direct basis. By dollar volume they now account for over half of the number of shares owned in this country, and they are customers as well for many of the other products sold by brokers.

But we also talked of the so-called institutional shareholders. These are financial institutions—banks, insurance companies, mutual funds, pension and profit-sharing funds, and other such organizations. In many ways, they are the securities industry's wholesale customers, as they hold shares on behalf of others or for the ultimate benefit of others. The bank trust department holds shares in trust for its customers who are still living, or for their estates, or for pension plans that will one day benefit individuals covered by the plan. Insurance companies invest in shares for the same reason, and also put their premium dollars to work in this way. Mutual funds are pooled institutional holdings of shares, an interest in which in turn is owned by the individuals who purchase shares in the fund itself.

The increase in these institutional holdings in recent years has had important effects on the securities industry. More than half of its business, in dollars and in numbers of shares, is now done with institutions, who deal in far larger blocks of stock than the individual investor does. The effects of this gradual institutionalization of the marketplace, in fact, has had effects all the way back through the securities process—expanding the industry in some important ways, and both changing and broadening the nature and requirements of many of its key jobs. But added together, the individual and institutional shareholders make up the marketplace of the securities industry. They are the source of the capital it provides to the economy—and of an important part of the industry's own income.

The securities "aftermarket" is just that: it is the industry's attention to its products after they have entered the marketplace. This attention is needed whether the product is an actual security, such as a stock, or another form of capital needed or held by a customer. Research, as we have seen, plays an important part in the aftermarket by continuing to evaluate each security's worth in the market. Once a security is issued, the firms that are interested in it take an active part in its later trading, both for their own accounts and for their customers. The managing underwriter, who sponsored the issue when it was first sold, is especially attentive to its future success. His reputation is at stake, and he continues to assist the company with any services that will help maintain and increase the value of its securities. Later, there may be opportunities for additional issues of stock, or for other forms of financing. Then the whole chain reaction begins again.

We have said several times that stocks and bonds are by no means the only "products" of the securities industry. This has become more and more true in recent years. Securities firms have aggressively diversified into broader lines of activity and new marketplaces. So, in fact, have other financial service industries like banking and insurance companies. The concept of the "financial supermarket" is a very real one today.

Some of this, of course, has been going on for years. Securities firms have long experience in the commodities business, which centers around dealings in present and future prices for such diverse items as foods like grains and meats, or metals like silver and platinum. This is a form of arbitrage—the taking advantage of distortions or differences between prices for the same item in different places at the same time, or, as in the "futures" market, at different times. Arbitrage, in fact, is another longtime activity in the securities business. It can be applied to price distortions between stocks and bonds in different marketplaces, or to the changing relationships in values between stocks that are going to be exchanged by two companies that are merging.

More recently, securities firms have entered into a number of different real estate activities. They finance the purchase and construction of properties like office buildings, shopping centers, and apartments. They make participation in such projects available to their customers. Leasing is another recent activity at securities firms —helping their customers gain the financial advantages of "renting" all kinds of things from road-building equipment to railroad cars, aircraft, and buildings, rather than having to bear the financial burden of outright ownership or purchase. The massive oceangoing tankers that carry energy products between continents today are being financed in this way, often by international teams of securities firms and other financial institutions.

Securities firms also develop and sell their own mutual funds today, in addition to their role in underwriting the issues of other funds. Some firms are also active in asset management—supervising the investment portfolios of pension funds, college endowment funds, profit-sharing trusts, and the holdings of other institutions. Asset management can be performed for large individual investors as well. Finally, one of the newest diversifications in the securities business is insurance. Firms now are selling policies on behalf of established insurance underwriters, but they are also looking into the possibility of underwriting the insurance themselves.

We have generally looked now at all of the kinds of things that securities firms do. The logical question at this point is: Can any one firm in the securities industry do all of that? The answer is probably that none of the firms, even the largest, engages in *all* of the activities of the securities industry. Of the 5,000 companies in the industry, it would be hard to find any two that had exactly the same business profile. The larger firms, of course, cover substantial segments of the industry's business spectrum. But even they differ greatly in emphasis from company to company.

One of the points that makes the securities industry a fascinating career choice, in fact, is the great number of kinds of firms it is possible to work for. Let us consider some of the categories, among both large and small firms, to give you an idea of both the diversity and the specialization that there is to choose from.

The Retail Firm

Retail firms are companies that are well known for their broad dealings with individual investors. They include many of the largest firms in the industry, but they can be very small as well. The large retail firms are generally well integrated in their services, dealing also with institutions and functioning as investment bankers as well as in many other securities product and service areas. The largest securities firm of all—Merrill, Lynch, Pierce, Fenner & Smith, Inc.—is also the largest retail house, with over 1,250,000 individual accounts. Other large retailers of securities are Bache & Co., Inc., Dean Witter & Co., Inc., and E. F. Hutton & Company, Inc., with several hundreds of thousands of accounts. In contrast, there are small new firms such as Black Stein Kimball, Inc., in Paramus, New Jersey. It has just 2,500 accounts—but it is no less dedicated to the retail market in securities.

The Institutional Firm

Here the emphasis is on the nonindividual investor—the large financial institutions that now account for more than half of the securities marketplace. They are less well known to the public, perhaps, but some of them are no less substantial in size. Salomon Brothers, an entirely institutional firm, is second only to Merrill Lynch in the total amount of capital that the firm has to do business with, and it uses this capital to take investment positions in some of the largest blocks of stock that are traded in Wall Street. Loeb, Rhoades & Co., Goldman, Sachs & Co., and First Boston Corporation, all primarily institutional firms, are also all among the top ten securities firms in the industry.

The Bond Firm

Many firms specialize in debt securities: corporate bonds and those of governments and government agencies. Their services cover the range from research to sales and market-making—but only in bonds. John Nuveen & Co., Inc., is one leading bond house. And some firms deal only in particular types of bonds. Carroll, McEntee & McGinley, Inc., specializes in U.S. government debt securities.

The Research Firm

One of the relatively new specialties in the industry is securities analysis. This can also be one of the most interesting and well-paying jobs, for its services are in demand throughout the industry, and some firms do the bulk of their business by providing research to other securities companies. William D. Witter, Inc., is one example of a firm specializing primarily in research services.

The Underwriting Firm

Underwriting, or investment banking, is one of the broadest specialties in the industry, and there is a trend today toward more and more firms taking an active role in bringing new securities to market. Many very prestigious firms, like Morgan Stanley & Co., Inc., and Lehman Brothers, Inc., are known largely for their skills in underwriting.

The New Issue Firm

After securities have been underwritten and brought to market, some firms specialize in trading these stocks during the early period of their public ownership when their price action can provide interesting and profitable opportunities. One such firm is A. P. Montgomery & Co., Inc.

The Over-the-Counter Firm

As the name implies, there are firms that trade only in unlisted securities that are not traded on exchanges. The thousands and thousands of unlisted securities include many new and emerging companies—but also some of the longest established businesses in America. Until recently, bank stocks stayed chiefly in the OTC market, and firms like Keefe, Bruyette & Woods, Inc., and M. A. Schapiro & Co., Inc., grew up to serve the growing markets for these securities. Another important over-the-counter firm is Troster, Singer & Co. There are also the so-called "third market" firms that trade listed stocks in the over-the-counter market. Weeden & Co. is one of the largest such firms.

The Odd-Lot Firm

The common trading unit in securities is 100 shares, known as a "round lot." But small investors and others also buy and sell shares in "odd lots" of fewer than 100 shares, and a firm—like Carlisle DeCoppet & Co.—is set up primarily to deal with other brokers in handling these odd-lot transactions.

The Specialist Firm

That's right. Among all the other specialties in Wall Street, there is one that is actually called a "specialist." These firms serve a unique function at the very heart of the securities marketplace. They work on the trading floors of the exchanges, and they are registered to trade in particular stocks on a long-term basis. Their role is to maintain an orderly market by buying and selling stocks for their own account to keep the supply and demand of a stock as much in balance as possible. The purpose of this is to keep prices from fluctuating violently when there is heavy buying or heavy selling—this assures the investor of a ready and reasonable market for the shares he holds. Specialists also act as brokers for other brokers who cannot always be on the exchange floor, and the specialists make their income on commissions from this business as well as from their own trading back and forth in the long-term positions they hold in the stocks they represent. Examples of specialist firms are Wagner, Strott &

Co., which makes markets in Xerox, Gulf Oil, and CNA Financial among other stocks, and Adler, Coleman & Co., which handles Motorola and Avon Products.

The Block-Positioning Firm

Firms that specialize in trading large blocks of stock have grown up in response to an increasingly institutional market, where stock is bought and sold in single chunks of hundreds of thousands of shares worth as much as $50,000,000 or $100,000,000 in one trade. To hold positions of this size requires large and well-capitalized firms and skillful trading instincts. The best-known firms in block trading are Salomon Brothers, and Goldman, Sachs.

The Commodities Firm

Commodities are a particularly sophisticated discipline. This specialty is practiced by some of the largest firms like Merrill Lynch, Bache, and E. F. Hutton as well as by firms that deal exclusively in metals or grain or coffee. Separate exchanges also are set up to deal only in commodities, such as the New York Coffee and Sugar Exchange, and the Chicago Board of Trade.

The Arbitrage Firm

Arbitrage, as we have noted, is the trading in price differentials of securities, although the technique can also be applied to currencies or, for that matter, to commodities. Securities arbitrage is practiced by a relatively few firms—Goldman, Sachs is an example—and often is done for the firm's own account rather than for those of customers. A recent trend is international securities arbitrage, where stocks may trade at different levels in different countries.

The Regional Firm

We mentioned examples of regional firms earlier. Here the specialty is often geographic—applied to a particular part of the country rather than a particular kind of business or a business with national coverage. A regional firm can offer a wide range of services, and it has the advantage of being close to its local investors, companies, industries, and institutions. Often, in such areas as underwriting, the regional firm will help a local company through its early growth and then later ally itself with larger firms when the time is right for a major issue of stock.

The Correspondent Firm

Some firms in the securities industry make a specialty of providing services to other firms that do not have their own offices in the same cities. The correspondent firm is often located in the major money centers like New York, and its relationships are with regional firms that do not have a New York presence. Pershing & Co., Inc., in New York, a good-sized firm in its own right, acts as correspondent for many regionals besides conducting its own business.

Clearly, the securities industry is a diverse place to work. The companies within the industry—as well as their marketplaces, the exchanges—have individual profiles and personalities. And it is probably obvious to you by now that there is no lack of different jobs to choose and train for. Now we shall look at some of those jobs—and how to prepare for them.

CHAPTER V

Who Works in Wall Street?

There's always a key question for anyone seeking a job. Is this career field open to me? It is a question that has traditionally applied to the young and inexperienced. Can I get a job in this industry if I'm just out of high school or college? Supposing I have just a high-school education? In either case, what kind of educational training should I make sure to bring with me?

Today, with more social awareness in all business affairs, the question has some broader implications. Regardless of my educational background, what if I'm a black? What if I'm a woman?

All right, let us suppose you are young, black, and/or female. What are your prospects in the securities industry? Let us take them one by one.

The Youth Movement

In securities, like any industry, age qualifications have evolved over the history of this long-established business. In more modern times, perhaps, seniority in years has been a ruling factor. And the more formal education a person had, the better the prospects for employment in the first place and advancement later on. This, though,

Lunch hour on Wall Street.

may have been more characteristic of a passing period in the industry, and one that was shared with many other industries. It is not so true today. The need for talent throughout business has broadened and "informalized" job standards that once were more rigid.

Remember, too, that it has not been too many decades since college education became widely available to Americans. Even today, a survey of the securities industry's senior managers would show a great many in top positions who had not attended or finished college. They went to work in Wall Street at a very early age and rose through their organizations on the basis of training and experience in a succession of jobs. Often, they added to their formal education as they went along. For that matter, this is a practice followed by many individuals who begin a business career equipped even with graduate degrees.

Opportunities for persons with less than a college degree have always existed in securities companies, and they do today. Admittedly, they are likely to be the lower-paying, clerical sorts of jobs. But they do exist in abundance, as we shall see in a later chapter, and they can be a solid beginning for the person willing to take the initiative to learn, take advantage of training programs and educational courses on the side, and qualify for broader, better-paid jobs later.

For the new job-seeker, even with a college degree, there are areas of the securities business that are likely to be closed off initially for reasons of lack of experience. The intricacies of complex fields like arbitrage, commodities, syndicate management, and investment banking are often beyond the brand-new jobholder. The risks that a securities company takes with its own capital and that of its investors in these kinds of work will generally rule against on-the-job training for a completely inexperienced person.

Even here, though, the prospects for early experience in some of Wall Street's more sophisticated disciplines seem to be improving. One clear trend is the sharply rising interest among business students in entrepreneurship—the starting of new companies and the management of young companies in contrast to seeking and holding a job in an established corporation. Courses in entrepreneurship and venture capitalism are becoming more widely available in colleges and universities. And, as we have seen, venture capital is often the first stage in the corporate finance and investment banking activities of a securities firm. Stock investing courses, too, as early as the high-school level, are providing students with practical experience in securities subjects that once scarcely were taught even in colleges.

Happily for new job-seekers, the largest single job category in the securities industry—the stockbroker, account executive, or registered representative—is increasingly open to new graduates. Here again, though, it is only realistic to note that experience counts in this field as it does everywhere. Most firms probably still prefer their candidates for these jobs to have some experience or training in sales already—or to be experienced in some other area of the securities business, such as research or trading. But some firms are opening their sales training programs to graduates, especially those with an M.B.A. degree, who show in testing that they have the early instincts of an effective salesperson.

If this is happening today, it is not entirely new in the securities industry. Yes, there have been times in Wall Street when it seemed that people did not hold important jobs unless they had gray in their hair, an impeccable prep-school and college pedigree, and twenty years of experience. This is not true today, and Wall Street offers numerous cases of young men who made a mark very early. Some examples:

• The firm of Donaldson, Lufkin & Jenrette, Inc., was founded in 1959 by three young men in their 20's with degrees from the Harvard Graduate School of Business Administration and only a few years of experience each under their belts. Each was a millionaire by the time he was 30, and the firm today is close to being one of the ten largest in the securities industry.

• Alger B. Chapman, Jr., 35, is president of Shearson, Hammill & Co., Inc., which *is* one of the ten largest brokerage firms. Before he joined Shearson in his 20's, Chapman was vice-president for legal affairs of the New York Stock Exchange.

• Morton H. Meyerson, 32, is president of duPont Glore Forgan, Inc., the industry's third-largest firm in commission business. Before joining duPont, Meyerson was a vice-president of Electronic Data Systems, Inc., a Dallas-based computer services company that owns a substantial interest in duPont.

• At E. F. Hutton & Co., Inc., another of the top ten brokers, the executives in charge of sales, planning, and syndication are all men in their mid-30's. Similar key jobs at other firms are held by increasingly younger men.

• At Merrill Lynch, Pierce, Fenner & Smith, Inc., the largest company in the industry, the leading securities salesman in 1972 was 39-year-old David A. Stulberg, who has been doing this kind of work in the firm's Detroit office since 1960, when he was 27. Stulberg's pay as a registered representative in 1972 was $295,000—

more than the chairman and chief executive of Merrill Lynch earned.

• In 1971, the chairman of the board of governors of the New York Stock Exchange was Ralph D. DeNunzio, then 39 and already executive vice-president of Kidder, Peabody & Co., Inc. The vice-chairman of the exchange that same year was Stephen M. Peck, then 36 and the managing partner of the specialist firm of Weiss, Peck & Greer. Peck, in fact, first became a specialist on the floor of the exchange at the age of 21.

• And, the full-time president of the National Stock Exchange, the smallest of the three in New York, is John D. Girard, who was 29 when named to the job and had already been with the NSE for four years, most recently as the vice-president in charge of qualifying stocks for listing on the exchange.

The Minority Report

Wall Street's opportunities for blacks are far newer than any discernible youth movement. But the 1970's are bringing a change in this social imbalance. Historically, again, there have been clerical jobs open to minority employees—but few openings much above clerical positions or salary scales. Now, there are. And, as black capitalism grows both in its scope and degree of success throughout the business world, opportunities in the financial marketplaces can be expected to grow as well.

At present, two New York Stock Exchange member firms are owned and operated by blacks: Daniels & Bell, Inc., and First Harlem Securities Corporation. Both firms were formed in 1971, and each firm holds two seats on the New York Stock Exchange, which in turn allows each firm to have two traders on the exchange floor.

Daniels & Bell was founded by Willie L. Daniels, 35, and Travers J. Bell, Jr., 32, both college graduates. The firm has concentrated on research and institutional business in Wall Street's primary marketplaces rather than the development of a black clientele. Its second seat on the exchange was purchased this year for Frank Quintana, a 30-year-old Puerto Rican, not a college graduate, who worked seven years for Salomon Brothers as a Teletype operator and clerk on the preferred stock desk.

The founder of First Harlem Securities was Russell Goings, who had been a linebacker for the Buffalo Bills, and who once shined shoes in Wall Street. First Harlem also specializes in institutional business, and one of its floor members on the exchange is 30-year-old Irvin W. Hanks, a graduate of the Stanford Graduate School of Business.

Wall Street's major firms are making efforts to broaden management and sales jobs for minorities. Last year, approximately 100 of the 1,800 sales representatives at Bache & Co., one of the industry's top three firms, were blacks, Orientals, American Indians, Spanish-surnamed persons—and women. Wylie H. Whisonant, Jr., a black who manages Bache's Rockefeller Center office, sold securities in the firm's Washington, D.C., office for eight years, and is recruiting additional black salesmen for Bache. The firm's program to bring blacks into sales

WOMEN EMPLOYED BY SECURITIES DEALERS AND EXCHANGES

	1960	*1965*	*1971*	*1972#*	*1973**	*1975**	*1978**	*1980**
Total employees	113,115	128,662	197,647	205,714	211,000	224,000	244,000	259,000
Women employees	34,500	40,400	67,200	72,000	75,116	82,208	93,940	102,823
Women as a % of total	30.5%	31.4%	34.0%	35.0%	35.6%	36.7%	38.5%	39.7%

1972 estimates were furnished by Mary Kramer, U.S. Department of Labor, Women's Bureau.

* Projections of total employment are from the National Planning Association, Washington, D.C.

Projections of women employees are a straight line extrapolation of the 1960–1972 growth in their share of total employment.

SOURCE : U.S. Department of Labor, Women's Bureau.
National Planning Association, *Report No. 70-N-1*, *Economic Projections Series; Report No. 68-N-1;* and *Report No. 66-R-1.*

and management poses standards that are high, but flexible. An applicant should have a college degree, but this is not essential. Some business experience is expected, preferably in sales.

Other firms have similar programs. Alonzo V. Wallette, a black, was an employee relations manager for

(Left) *Shirley Chilton, managing partner of a member firm of the New York Stock Exchange.* (Right) *Jean Dunne, of Gilligan, Will & Co., in 1972 became an accredited stock specialist on the National Stock Exchange, the first woman specialist in the history of securities trading in the United States.*

Electronic Data Systems before he became vice-president for administration at duPont Glore Forgan. His job includes personnel as well as communications and management of the firm's office leases. Wallette's ambition is not only to extend minority opportunities above the clerical ranks at duPont Glore Forgan, but also to put the entire firm on a "classless" basis in terms of benefits and rewards for performance over seniority.

The Liberation of Wall Street's Women

"There are two paths where women are forbidden to tread—aboard ships and on Wall Street. And in times of crisis, they are permitted aboard ship!"

This may not be very amusing in Women's Lib circles today, but it is cited by one Wall Street personnel executive as the attitude that once prevailed in the securities industry. Not so today. On a comparable basis, at least, Wall Street is keeping pace with the rest of American business in providing more and better career opportunities for women. In fact, with the possible exception of some of the communications industries—publishing, advertising, and public relations—women in Wall Street are achieving more stature and responsibility in a broader range of jobs than in any other business.

There are statistics to show the gains women have made. As we have seen, the securities industry employs somewhat more than 200,000 people, and about one third of these today are women, according to estimates by the U.S. Department of Labor and the National Planning Association. By far the largest part of these jobs still are secretarial and clerical: stenographers and typists, bookkeepers, keypunch operators in the industry's growing electronic areas. The growth in Wall Street's data processing volume, in fact, has added an expanding professional need for women, as well as men, who are trained as computer programmers.

In the industry's more established professional areas, women are taking more and more of the better jobs. As early as 1968, of the New York Stock Exchange community's 49,644 registered representatives—its securities salespeople—3,056 were women. Today, while the total number of stockbrokers has risen less than 10 percent, nearly 70 percent more women—or more than 5,000—hold these jobs.

Early this year, 22-year-old Mrs. Jean Dunne became a specialist on the National Stock Exchange—probably the first woman to work as a specialist, or market maker, on any American exchange. Mrs. Dunne is the third generation of her family to do business on the NSE, and her experience, since the age of 17, has been in jobs with her family's brokerage firm and as a wire clerk at the American Stock Exchange.

Research, another of the securities industry's areas of highest employment and the best-paying jobs, is also providing a rising proportion of women's jobs in Wall Street. Security analysts do their work on a specialized basis that runs the gamut of every industry in American business, and a check of the Financial Analysts Federation membership directory shows women analysts in every field from aerospace and automobiles through banking and bonds to steel, transportation, and utilities. If there was a day when female analysts were limited to fields like retailing, cosmetics, home furnishings, and textiles and apparel, it has passed. As just one example, Isabel H. Benham at Shearson, Hammill is widely conceded to be the ranking railroad analyst in Wall Street.

The 1968 figures of the New York Stock Exchange also showed that women held more than a fourth of the limited partnerships—387 out of 1,444 such positions—in exchange member firms. Today, while the partnership form of doing business in Wall Street is changing to the corporate form, it is no longer startling to find women in a securities firm's most senior jobs.

Julia Montgomery Walsh, 49, joined Ferris & Co. in 1955 and was named a general partner in 1969; she is now a senior vice-president of the incorporated firm. Mrs. Walsh, who has handled some of her company's most prestigious clients at its home office in Washington, D.C., was one of the first two women elected to membership on the American Stock Exchange, in 1965, and more recently was the first woman from the industry to serve as a director of that exchange. She now has a new title—"exchange official"—and is the first woman to hold this position, created by the American exchange for its industry committee members.

The first woman to buy a membership on the New York Stock Exchange was Muriel Siebert, who has headed her own successful firm, Muriel Siebert & Co., Inc., since 1967. One of Shirley R. Chilton's first jobs was as a switchboard operator at the West Coast securities firm of Daniel Reeves & Co.; recently, Mrs. Chilton headed a group that bought control of the company. In the interim, Mrs. Chilton had become a registered representative, and held top jobs at Hayden, Stone & Co., and William O'Neil & Co., Inc.

In one securities area after another, then, women are

gaining representation. There is, unfortunately, still some disparity in salaries for women and men holding the same jobs in some securities disciplines. And there is still a special effort to be made by a woman, in many cases, to gain the better jobs in the first place, and then to gain acceptance for her work. But in Wall Street, as elsewhere, performance is what counts. And at that level—for women as well as men—the battle of the sexes is over.

CHAPTER VI

A Closer Look at Some Securities Jobs

The securities industry as a place to work is one of great variety. The companies in the industry—as well as their marketplaces, the exchanges—have individual profiles and personalities. No two are apt to be alike in purpose or practice. And it is obvious by now that there are dozens of different jobs to choose from and train for. Again, jobs even of the same sort will differ from company to company and market to market. But there are general patterns that offer enough detail to guide you as a job-seeker in deciding where the most interesting work may be for you.

We have also seen that many securities jobs require college training, while others are open to the high-school graduate. Here is a summary of four different jobs in detail. Two of them—the broker and the security analyst—normally call for college work. Two others—the order clerk and the margin clerk—do not.

The Broker

Here again is our most familiar securities industry employee—the man or woman who advises investors on their investments and places the orders to buy or sell

COURTESY PAINE, WEBBER, JACKSON & CURTIS

Stockbroker trainees of a New York Stock Exchange member firm attend one of numerous sessions in the home office in New York City.

stocks, bonds, and the other products or services for a securities firm's customers. This job goes under several titles: securities broker, account executive, or registered representative. In a member firm of the New York Stock Exchange, the last title is used, and it means that the person must meet the requirements of the exchange before he or she is permitted to deal with the public.

The registered representative undergoes training for a minimum of six months; at some firms, the training lasts for nine months or a year. Whether the program is conducted by the prospective broker's own firm, or at accredited outside schools, the training cycle will include courses in a good many of the subjects we have been talking about: accounting, corporate and municipal bonds, corporate finance, equity and fixed-income securities, financial statements, institutional sales, margin regulations, money markets, mutual funds, over-the-counter markets, public speaking, sales techniques, securities law, securities analysis, and underwriting. At the end of this training, in a New York Stock Exchange member firm, the broker must pass qualifying examinations given by the exchange.

The broker's job is a central one in a securities firm. As a member of the sales department, the broker is in an area that is responsible for important portions of the overall revenue of the firm, as well as its profits. As one link in the capital formation process, brokers help to sell the products of their firm's own underwriting departments, as well as all issues in which the firm participates and all securities in which the firm makes markets. In many firms, income-producing activities extend well beyond the basic stock and bond investments, and some brokers deal also in investment funds, options, commodities, real estate participations, and insurance.

What kind of person makes a good broker? In today's markets, the ideal broker has a strong grounding in sales, financial skills, and management. Initiative and self-motivation are his key traits. Sales experience is helpful because it implies skill in dealing with people. Many account executive training programs seek candidates who have a successful track record in sales work for companies like IBM or Xerox. But candidates also qualify who can demonstrate sales aptitudes without having had actual experience. If an M.B.A. graduate whose studies

COURTESY PAINE, WEBBER, JACKSON & CURTIS

All securities processed in major brokerage firms are photographed as a safety precaution.

or interests have included finance and management can convince a brokerage firm of his maturity of judgment and his sales instincts, he may be accepted for the firm's training program.

Many firms feel that 25 or 26 is the "age of experience" for a prospective broker. Successful brokerage is a matter both of gaining and justifying the confidence of investors, and some initial experience—even at the college level—is useful in creating such sales relationships. This is why the graduate student, the experienced salesperson, and others with some exposure to business experience are more welcome at securities firms. Another area of experience that has led to securities careers is the military, where both newly retired and younger personnel have demonstrated the qualities of confidence, leadership, and ability in person-to-person relationships that a broker needs.

The Security Analyst

The broker is expected to be continually informed about industries, companies, stocks, and business trends of current and potential interest to his customers. Much of this information results from his own studies, but the broker also relies heavily on research provided his firm, by other firms that specialize in research services, or both. This research is the job of the security analyst.

The analyst performs a formidable job of information-seeking and evaluation. He must ask the right questions, weigh the answers, sift through reams of reports and statistics, and make reasoned judgments from all of this as to what securities should be bought, sold, or held—or which of all the other possible investment options are the most favorable at any given time.

The questions are infinite, and range from broad economic matters to the most specific details about a single company. Will the economy continue to expand, and at what rate? Will there be a recession, and how long might it last? How will business be affected by the government's policies toward prices, wages and labor negotiations, mergers, patents, and overseas investment? What effect will these have on the stock market, and what will be the impact on the values of individual securities? Is an industry growing or stagnant? Which are the best- and worst-situated companies in an industry group? What will a specific company's earnings be next quarter, at the end of the year, in two years, or in five years? What will a new product or acquisition contribute to earnings? How will all of this affect the ratio of a company's earnings to its price in the market? Do earnings seem overvalued, undervalued, or reasonably valued at current market prices?

The ability to deal intelligently with these and many other similar questions determines the analyst's skill in making the right recommendations. He is only human, and the marketplace is always ready to expose his fallibility. But the work is challenging, never routine, and as varied as the business world it studies.

Analysts, like brokers, may come from a variety of backgrounds. A common thread, though, is likely to be in training or experience in economics, business, and finance. Many analysts have graduate degrees, and many have come into the field from earlier careers in law, engineering, accounting, journalism, teaching, and sales. College work will have been in such subjects as accounting, business administration, economics, and financial statistics and analysis. The analyst will understand both the uses and limitations of statistics, and he will have a thorough understanding of the workings of securities markets.

Most security analysts specialize in an industry or in several related industries. An analyst may cover the steel industry along with other industries that consume great quantities of steel—such as automobiles and farm equipment. Aerospace and electronics go together. So do chem-

COURTESY PAINE, WEBBER, JACKSON & CURTIS

(Left) *The stock record department of a New York Stock Exchange member firm provides immediate reference to determine which customers own stock in a specific corporation.* (Right) *Operations clerks check securities in the process of handling in major brokerage houses.*

icals, drugs, and cosmetics, or printing and publishing, or textiles and apparel.

Knowing his industries in detail is a must for the analyst. The typical analyst travels often to call on the companies he covers, cultivating close relationships with their executives, and investigating firsthand the conditions in the industry. This done, his next task is to piece together all that he has learned, and present it to his brokers and outside customers in a lucid and logical written report. Often, as well, he will find himself "talking" his conclusions to clients and his own associates. So the ability to think and speak on his feet is also useful.

For his considerable skills, a good analyst is well paid.

And, a career that is interesting and profitable of itself can also lead to later jobs in sales and management.

The Order Clerk

When the broker, wherever he is, puts through his client's instructions to buy or sell shares of stock, these are transmitted to the order room of the firm's main office. Now the order clerk takes over. Generally, this employee is a high-school graduate with an interest or ability in clerical skills. Prospective order clerks, after they are hired, are given a period of orientation and on-the-job training by the firm.

When he receives the broker's order, the order clerk uses a direct line to telephone the firm's phone clerk on the floor of the exchange and relay the order to him. Then, when the order has been executed on the exchange floor by the firm's floor broker, the phone clerk calls back to the order clerk to confirm the transaction to him. The order clerk in turn relays the confirmation back to the original broker by Teletype, and the broker informs the client of the terms of the trade he has made.

Meanwhile, the order clerk is making out a "house report" on the transaction. This includes the name of the investor, the broker, and the stock involved, as well as the number of shares traded, the price paid or collected, and other related information. The house report is used by other employees of the firm to figure the commission, bill the client, transfer ownership of the stock, and provide accounting records of the transaction for the firm.

The order clerk's job can be hectic, and he must be

able to work under pressure. He is often involved in multiple transactions at the same time, and he must be able to handle these with speed and accuracy. While in the midst of one transaction or house report, he may also receive more orders and more confirmations, and he must be able to keep them all straight and in motion.

Order clerks are employed by firms operating on the major exchanges as well as the regional exchanges. A variation of the order clerk's job is found in commodities trading on these specialized exchanges. One logical promotion route for a skilled order clerk is to the floor broker's job—the firm's partner or officer who executes orders on the exchange floor.

The Margin Clerk

Another clerical specialty comes into play when investors "buy on margin"—one of many variations that a securities transaction can take. In effect, an investor may purchase securities on credit, although he must pay for a portion of the stock immediately on purchase. The percent of the purchase price to be paid right away is determined by the Federal Reserve Board, and it has varied over the years from 40 percent to 100 percent depending on market conditions.

The margin clerk may also be a high-school graduate, and this time he is likely to be a person with an aptitude for mathematics. His job is to be sure that margin accounts conform at all times to the regulations of the government and of the stock exchanges. The margin clerk may be located in any one of a firm's offices, and main-

COURTESY MERRILL LYNCH, PIERCE, FENNER & SMITH

In a New York Stock Exchange member firm office, an account executive discusses investment strategy on the telephone while another prepares to place an order.

tains there the margin file on each customer who does business with the office, entering there the confirmations of each trade.

When the price of a margin-purchased stock goes up, the margin clerk and his firm have no reason to be concerned. An investor may then sell his stock at a profit, using part of the proceeds to pay the firm the amount he still owes. If the stock's price goes down, however, the customer's margin may exceed the percentage in force at that time. The margin clerk must continually recalculate each investor's margin status, ready to notify him when additional funds or stock are needed to fulfill current margin regulations.

A margin clerk will be in charge of numerous accounts, and in large firms there may be many margin clerks watching thousands of accounts. The margin clerk must be accurate in his calculations, and quick to stay ahead of the market's shifting prices. His job, like the order clerk's, cannot be delayed. Stock prices can change within minutes, and the firm that allows its customers to exceed margin rules will itself be penalized by having to "buy in" the offending securities—a penalty that can result in large financial losses to the firm.

A margin clerk may begin with a firm in more routine clerical jobs. And, like the order clerk, he may also work up to more advanced areas. The financial skills and quickness that are demanded of a margin clerk, for instance, have also found applications in a securities firm's research department, or on its arbitrage desk.

CHAPTER VII

Wall Street Jobs—and What They Pay

It is time we zeroed in on that very practical question: How much can I earn in the securities industry?

Some Wall Street jobs pay very well indeed—depending, though, very much on performance. Perhaps more than in many other industries, securities jobs are scaled frequently on an incentive basis rather than on straight salary measures. This may apply more to the advanced jobs in terms of salaries, commissions, and bonuses. But at many firms, the bonus system is a factor in all jobs. And, at these levels, the incentives are in the form of possible promotion to more responsible work at better pay. The sheer diversity of Wall Street work makes this possible, and it creates a situation of exciting potential for the ambitious new employee.

Here are general summaries of the categories of jobs to be found in a brokerage firm. Included are the starting salaries of such positions in the New York area, and the projected earnings potential of each job. The first eleven job areas are examples of those that call for more educational background and working experience. Then we shall look at ten job areas that do not require a college degree.

Starting salaries for the higher positions in Wall Street are pegged more flexibly to the individual applicant. Securities firms must be competitive with each other—but as firms differ in their profiles and specialties, so do their job definitions. Salaries are thus set on a combination of

Through electronic equipment, brokers get an immediate quotation on a stock in which they are interested.

the duties a firm wants performed and the background a person brings to the job. Sales commissions, for instance, may be set at various rates for varying volumes of accounts. And, of two applicants for the same job, the person with more educational background and/or experience in the work may expect a higher starting salary.

Account Executive

We have already looked at the varied backgrounds and experience that produce many Wall Street brokers, account executives, and registered representatives. More than any other employee in the securities industry, a good account executive has almost unlimited earning potential. His income depends very much on his ability. But it also depends on the performance of the stock market. Thus the income of the account executive, like that of salespeople in many fields, can vary widely from year to year.

Most account executives are paid a commission on every transaction they handle. This can range from 17 percent to 40 percent of the total commission the firm receives from a customer, depending again on the broker's volume and the firm's policies. In some firms, registered representatives are paid a straight salary and a bonus calculated both on his performance and the overall results of the firm's business.

Initially, in a training program, the prospective account executive earns about $750 a month. On the job, as experience grows, his income can reach $50,000 to $100,000 a year. And, as we have seen from the experience of David Stulberg at Merrill Lynch last year, registered representatives have been known to earn $300,000 a year—and even higher.

Accounting

A securities firm's accounting department may be divided into four areas of responsibility:

1. The balance sheet section watches over the general financial condition of the firm.
2. The income and expense section keeps track of money owed to the firm and owed by the firm.
3. The office accounting section is responsible for the cash and securities that must be transferred between the firm's offices.
4. The payroll section is responsible for payment of the firm's employees.

The educational credentials for jobs in securities accounting include bachelor's and master's degrees in accounting itself and in business administration. Starting salaries today are in the $8,500 range, and the potential earning power is $25,000 to $50,000 for the top managerial positions in the field.

Auditing

The auditing department designs and evaluates a firm's internal accounting, financial, and operating controls—an area that securities firms are paying closer attention to, and for which talented employees today are much more in demand.

Educational requirements are similar to those in the accounting area: a B.A., M.A., or M.B.A. degree in accounting or business administration.

Salaries currently begin at $10,000 and can reach $50,000 for the top auditing jobs.

Commodities Research

This field, which is also of broader interest to securities firms today, is a specialized form of analysis focused on the major industrial and agricultural commodities, from precious metals to grains and other foodstuffs. The commodities analyst forecasts prices based on everything from economic supply and demand to weather conditions. Like his counterpart in security analysis, the commodity analyst specializes in related groups of commodities.

The education for commodities research can be quite varied, with both undergraduate and graduate degree sequences available in general economic and marketing as well as the agricultural specialties themselves.

Salaries in this area begin at $10,000.

Commodities Sales

The commodities salesperson carries out the orders of investors in the commodities futures markets, as part of an economic process that transfers price risk from the producer and the consumer to the investment marketplaces. Commodities sales may be a specialty, or it may be included in the skills of the more general registered representative. The transactions themselves take place on special exchanges.

Education: Similar to the commodities analyst.

Starting salaries: $8,000 to $12,000.

Corporate Planning

This is another of the securities industry's newly important areas, and as such the planning manager is in current demand. His job is to project the firm's future courses of possible action in relation to the industry's trends, acting as a "think tank" and information source for the firm's top management.

Education will include a liberal arts background that is intended to be the base for graduate study in business, management, and marketing.

Starting salaries will be in the range of $10,000 to $15,000.

Electronic Data Processing

These jobs will be found in a firm's Operations Division—responsible for the processing of all daily transactions, the maintenance of accurate and up-to-date records, and the providing of sales and marketing support data such as portfolio analysis, bond yield computations, and other computerized services.

Education may be a bachelor's degree in computer sciences and mathematics.

Salaries begin at $12,500 with an earning potential of $25,000 to $50,000.

Market Planning

This department of a securities firm works closely with Corporate Planning, but attacks a different set of questions. What markets should the firm be in? What products and services can be sold in these markets? Who are the logical customers? What will be the return to the firm? How should this new activity be staffed, supported, and promoted?

Educational background will include an undergraduate business degree and graduate study in management and marketing.

Starting salaries will range from $8,000 to $15,000.

Operations Management

This department sets guidelines for the entire Operations Division, including all clerical, accounting, and bookkeeping functions performed in all of the firm's offices, and supervision of the firm's overall financial controls.

Education will be in economics, finance, and management on the undergraduate level, and business administration on the graduate level.

Salaries will begin at $9,000, and potential earnings can reach $40,000 to $70,000 for senior operations managers.

Portfolio Management

Portfolio managers work with individual customers, relating the investor's specific goals with the securities and other investment vehicles whose characteristics are appropriate to reaching those particular goals.

Education may include economics, finance, and business administration on both the undergraduate and graduate levels.

Salaries in this sales-related field begin at $13,500 and have a potential of $25,000 to $30,000 in fifteen years. For the top jobs in portfolio management, salaries of $50,000 to $100,000 are possible.

Security Analysis

As we noted earlier, the analyst's job requires skills ranging from investigation to the synthesis of information and its orderly presentation. He must be part reporter, part economist, and part communicator.

Educational backgrounds also can cover a broad array of disciplines, but a basic education for analytical work will include accounting, economics, finance, and business administration.

Starting salaries for analysts will be at the $12,000 level, reaching $25,000 to $40,000 in fifteen years. Top analysts and reseach directors can command $50,000 to $100,000.

Here are ten positions common to most securities firms that do not call for college preparation. Listed are the basic duties of the job, whether firms normally provide training for the job, and rough guidelines as to initial and potential salaries.

Bookkeeper

Duties: Maintains the firm's financial records.
Training: Not in the basic skills of the job.
Salary: $125 per week; $145 after five years.

Box Clerk

Duties: Checks receipt and delivery of securities certificates against the firm's transaction records.

Training: Yes.

Salary: $115 per week to $160 per week depending on seniority.

Comparison Clerk

Duties: Compares information on order clerks' house reports with data from the exchange or other firms to assure that the stock, number of shares, and price paid in each transaction is correct.
Training: Yes.
Salary: $115 per week to $160 per week.

Figuration Clerk

Duties: Calculates the total price of a security being bought or sold, the taxes, and the commission to be charged.
Training: Yes.
Salary: Same as general clerical salaries.

Keypunch Operator

Duties: Operates a keypunch machine, similar to a typewriter, that transfers information to computer punchcards for data processing applications.
Training: Yes.
Salary: $115 per week to $145 per week with experience.

Margin Clerk

Duties: Price surveillance of margin accounts.
Training: Yes.
Salary: $115 per week to $190 per week depending on seniority.

Stock Record Clerk

Duties: Checks certificates to assure that they are acceptable for transfer of ownership, either as bought from a customer or sold to a customer. Checks share denomination and price paid against transaction record for accuracy.
Training: Yes.
Salary: General clerical salaries.

Secretary

Duties: Telephone, typing, dictation, filing, and general office duties.
Training: No.
Salary: $140 per week to a potential $185 per week.

Teletype Operator

Duties: Message transmission between brokerage offices, other firms, and customers. Sometimes, in small branch offices, this job is combined with the order clerk's job.
Training: Sometimes.
Salary: $120 per week to a potential $180 depending on seniority.

CHAPTER VIII

Ready to Go to Work?

First, Get the Job . . .

We have looked at what the securities industry does—its role in the business system and in the society. We have seen what kinds of jobs need to be done to fulfill that role. We have seen where the jobs are. We have talked in some detail about how to prepare for different kinds of jobs. We have looked at hiring practices. And we have looked at salary structures. Now—to turn all of this into an actual job. How do you do that?

With its hundreds of firms and dozens of specialties, the industry might seem an elusive target for a job-hunter. And that's all the more reason for you to have a good sense of Wall Street "geography"—where it's all at—as well as some sense of what areas of the industry's work are of particular interest to you. No, you are not likely to go directly into sales or investment banking or securities research in your first week on the job. But it will be useful if you have at least a good preliminary idea of which direction you would like to take.

Securities companies, in today's competitive business environment, are as much on the lookout for good people as you are for a good career. And they are mining a wide range of sources to meet their personnel needs. One recent industry study showed that employment agencies are the most frequently used sources; they account for almost half of all new employees—and more than half, it seems, in the case of smaller and medium-sized firms. Employment agencies generally charge a fee for placing people. But the same research shows that almost 90 percent of the time the company pays the fee outright; in the small minority of cases where the employee pays, he is usually reimbursed after a short probationary period.

Large firms, with their large work forces already in place, rely more on referrals from their own employees—a built-in recruiting department with widespread contacts in each specialty throughout the industry. And smaller firms do this as well, although necessarily in a more limited sense.

The large companies also make greater use of advertising to generate applicants than do their smaller counterparts. Good initial sources of job leads are the general classified sections of major newspapers—but the securities industry's ads are also likely to appear in newspaper business sections, in business newspapers like *The Wall Street Journal,* and in many magazines directed at the securities business. The magazines, if they do not carry employment advertising as such, will nonetheless give you clues in their articles about what activities dominate the marketplace at the moment, and which specialties are apt to be the current "hot" job markets. Trends develop and change quickly in this fast-paced industry, and an informed applicant can have an important advantage.

For that matter, it is a good overall rule—no matter how you gain a job interview—to teach yourself something about the company and its industry before you go in. Just reading an annual report, or looking up some financial data in Standard & Poor's *Corporate Directory* at the library, or finding some current articles on the subject will give you enough background to show that you are really interested.

Formal recruiting programs have also become more important for the brokers. With the industry's increasing interest in graduates who hold M.B.A degrees, campus recruiting is perhaps heaviest at graduate schools of business. But undergraduate recruiting is also done, particularly as colleges and universities develop more undergraduate business education programs. The same is true of technical schools that teach business skills. And high schools with vocational programs are also canvassed.

Direct application to a firm's personnel department is another route. As with companies in any industry, the larger the firm, the more complete its personnel functions will be. But every firm will have a partner or officer in charge of personnel administration, and this will often apply to the branch offices of firms as well. Even if you are a student still short of graduation, a visit to several firms may provide you with useful guidance on finishing up your studies with the best credentials for the time when you will actually be ready for employment.

When that day comes, take a good look at more than just the starting salaries and initial job responsibilities.

We shall have more to say shortly about the differences between a job and a career—an important distinction that applies especially in the securities industry. At the outset, though, do not overlook the area of fringe benefits. A full range of "fringes" is new enough in business life that the subject has almost become another symbol of the generation gap. The older hands, who began their careers without many benefits, may feel that newcomers overemphasize the subject. Do not be put off by this if you encounter it: Companies factor the cost of benefits into their own planning, and you should factor the benefits themselves into your evaluation of a job. Benefits represent money, and you will find that they can have a pronounced impact—good or bad—on your real earning power.

In the securities industry, for example, benefits can extend your actual wages by another 18 percent to 25 percent—sometimes even more. Benefit programs are viewed as an added way of attracting good people—and holding on to them. In common with most companies, the securities firms have the usual benefits like low-cost group life insurance, group medical and hospitalization plans, paid sick-leave provisions, and paid vacations and holidays. But they also, as an industry, make broader use of some of the more advanced fringe benefits and supplemental income plans. Research shows, for instance, that all but the smallest firms fund 100 percent of their retirement plans, without requiring an employee contribution. The industry also makes greater use of profit-sharing or thrift plans, for both exempt and nonexempt employees, and including the type of plan to which employees can contribute as a deferred income or savings device.

Cash bonuses are also more prevalent in the securities industry than in many other businesses. This is a policy that can vary both on an industrywide basis and from firm to firm at any given time, for it is tied very closely to business conditions, and firms also vary in their policies of relating bonuses to merit or performance. But overall, one industry study of some ninety firms, ranging from small to large, showed that in 1968—an upbeat year for the securities business in general—some 95 percent of all firms paid bonuses. In 1971—following a time when the industry's business had not been so favorable—the figures were down to 88 percent for small firms and 78 percent for large firms. By contrast, though, a similar study by the Commerce and Industry Association of New York showed that, of nearly 300 companies surveyed in a variety of industries, only a third were giving bonuses during that same period.

More recently, during a time of very mixed financial results among securities firms, the examples of three security analysts illustrate several points about bonuses. One analyst found that his firm had canceled all bonuses for the time being. Another was not only out his bonus, but experienced a 10 percent salary cut—and several of his fellow analysts were laid off. But the third, at exactly the same time, was paid a bonus that almost equaled his quarterly salary. It all proves, again: When you go to work, go to work for a winner.

This raises the question of job security in Wall Street. Historically, securities have been a cyclical business, closely tied to the national economy and its effect on investment markets. Economic recessions have led to temporary layoffs, salary reductions, and other unpleasant realities of traditional business life. It is one, moreover, that applied to high-salaried jobs as well as those that are not. But the rule in the securities business, as in most others, is that competence is the best form of job security you can have: A firm will make extra efforts to keep its better people, no matter what happens.

One plus factor for the future is the industry's diversification. By offering more services to its entire range of clients—from individual investors to large corporations and governments—the industry is combating its historical cyclicality. If the stock market is in a down trend, more defensive forms of investments become attractive. Life insurance and overall asset management are "product" areas whose trend lines can move counter to the dominant economic direction. The diversified financial services offered by the securities firm of the future is an effective form of job security for its employees.

. . . Now, Turn Your Job into a Career

If just getting a job and hanging on to it is your main goal, you may not be too happy in the competitive, self-motivating atmosphere of the securities industry.

Now that is a statement that any industry would like to make about itself. It also sounds ominously like a lead-in to the "pep talk" section that so many career books include in their pages. Not so here. This is not a manual on getting a haircut, what color shirt to wear, or how to sit in your chair during a job interview. Success, fulfillment, or whatever you want to call it is a more subtle and subjective matter than that.

The point rather is that the securities business, for all of its excitement and economic centrality—and perhaps because of these factors—is one of the more difficult businesses of our times. It is rapidly changing, growing more complicated with each change, and has a future as problematical as the business processes it serves. For all that we have been saying about good salaries, fringes, and the like—this is not an industry to consider in terms of a one-shot job tryout. The entry requirements for the better jobs are high. Your commitment, as you will have seen already, should have begun before you make application for your first job. Certainly, it will have to start as soon as you are employed.

Much of this, you will find, is built into the work itself. Apart from the educational credentials you bring to work on the first day, you will find that on-the-job training is widespread in the securities industry. We have seen that registered representatives—the securities salespeople—go through training programs from six months to as long as two years. Trainees are paid a salary, of course, but their real earning power does not appear until the training is completed. And the insistence on training is not whimsical on the part of the firms; it costs them too much for that. Successful completion of training, and the passing of certified examinations, is required by the New

Roster of Principal Organizations Active in the Securities & Investment Business

Organization

National Association of Securities Dealers, Inc.
1735 K Street N.W.
Washington, D.C. 20006
(202) 833–7200
Membership: 4,300

National *Security Traders* Association
120 Broadway
New York, New York 10005
(212) 697–6897
Membership: 32 Affiliates
5,000 Members

New York *Institute of Finance*
Two New York Plaza
New York, New York 10004
(212) 422–9835
Teaching Staff: 100

New York *Security Dealers* Association
26 Broadway
New York, New York 10004
(212) 344–1650
Membership: 100 Firms

New York Society of *Security Analysts,* Inc.
15 William Street
New York, New York 10005
(212) 944–3018–9
Membership: 4,979

Securities Industry Association
20 Broad Street
New York, New York 10005
(212) 425–2700

Security Traders' Association of New York, Inc.
79 Wall Street—Room 704
New York, New York 10005
(212) 344–0411
Membership: 1,150

Exchange

American Stock Exchange
86 Trinity Place
New York, New York 10006
(212) 938–6000
Membership: 650 Regular
207 Associate

Board of Trade of the City of Chicago
141 West Jackson Blvd.
Chicago, Illinois 60604
(312) 922–2800
Membership: 1,402

Boston Stock Exchange
53 State Street
Boston, Massachusetts 02109
(617) 723–9500
Membership: 196

Cincinnati Stock Exchange
205 Dixie Terminal Building
Cincinnati, Ohio 45202
(513) 621–1410
Membership: 30

Detroit Stock Exchange
2314 Penobscot Building
Detroit, Michigan 48226
(313) 963–1600
Membership: 60

Intermountain Stock Exchange
39 Exchange Place
Salt Lake City, Utah 84111
(801) 363–2531
Membership: 45

Midwest Stock Exchange
120 South LaSalle Street
Chicago, Illinois 60603
(312) 346–1111
Membership: 435

National Stock Exchange
91 Hudson Street
New York, New York 10013
(212) 966–6508
Membership: 175

New York Stock Exchange, Inc.
11 Wall Street
New York, New York 10005
(212) 623–3000
Membership: 1,366

Pacific Stock Exchange, Inc.
301 Pine Street
San Francisco, California 94106
(415) 392–6533
AND
618 South Spring Street
Los Angeles, California 90014
(213) 627–8741
Membership: 220

P-B-W Stock Exchange
17th Street and Stock Exchange Place
Philadelphia, Pennsylvania 19103
(215) 563–4700
Membership: 515

Spokane Stock Exchange
Peyton Building
Spokane, Washington 99201
(509) 624–4632
Membership: 15

York Stock Exchange for sales personnel of member firms, and by the National Association of Securities Dealers for over-the-counter securities sales. In 1972, the NASD administered some 65,000 examinations for its own members and for other organizations.

Other areas of the securities business are upgrading their professionalism along the same lines. For a salesman to work with customer accounts in commodities, for example, he must pass an examination developed by the Association of Commodity Exchange Firms and approved as well by the New York Stock Exchange. His branch manager must be registered as a commodities-knowledgeable person as well.

And, in security analysis, the Financial Analysts Federation sponsors a series of three examinations leading to the C.F.A. designation—Chartered Financial Analyst. Besides the rigorous exams, analysts going for the C.F.A. must also have been in this field of work for a prescribed number of years. While this kind of program, unlike the required training and exams for registered representatives, or the CPA for accountants, is not mandatory at present, there have been proposals for formal licensing of analysts. Meanwhile, the C.F.A. is a distinction—and a very complete education—that good analysts want to add to their credentials.

Many firms, particularly the larger ones, develop and conduct their own training programs for registered representatives, commodity salesmen, and other disciplines. Smaller firms use outside services for their training, and many firms combine the two methods. On-the-job training is also supplied, as we have seen, for a broad range of clerical jobs in securities firms, either preparing the new employee from scratch, or adding the firm's own methods to the employee's prior education.

There are few jobs of any kind today where the committed employee will not benefit by adding to his education with extra courses on the side—whether the subject is accounting, marketing, management, data processing, or many other areas of expertise. At colleges in larger cities that have concentrations of brokerage and underwriting firms, employees can often take the NYSE-approved course for registered representatives, or work with the business schools in their entrepreneurial education programs. Graduate schools of business offer a range of supplemental courses open to the off-hour employee.

Predictably, the New York area offers an unusual amount of supplemental education aimed at the securities business. The New York University Graduate School of Business Administration, on Trinity Place in lower Manhattan, is so close to the geographical heart of the industry that it has been called "a school for Wall Street." Pace University, near Wall Street, also provides a wide range of courses for those who want to be in the securities industry. Pace has the reputation of providing excellent courses. The New York Institute of Finance is also in the Wall Street area. Founded in 1922, it offers training programs for the industry as well as courses for the general public. Its teaching staff is drawn entirely from New York stock exchanges, securities firms, banks, and other nearby institutions. Industry trade and policy groups, such as the Securities Industry Association and the National Association of Securities Dealers, sponsor conferences and workshops for their members. And so do general business organizations like the American Management Association.

Securities firms will pay the tuition, usually all of it, for employees who take job-related courses. Supervisors will also counsel employees on the best way to add to their education, depending on the employee's goals and the firm's plans for him or her. Unlike some industries, the securities business is a vast collection of related but unranked disciplines. Today, unlike the past when sales work was often the route to the top, there is no single ladder of advancement, and changing of disciplines in midcareer is frequent. With proper training, an employee can readily switch fields without jeopardizing his prospects.

It should be clear by now how important self-motivation is to a successful career in securities. It is a quality that is sought in new employees. And the hope is that an employee will continue to "regenerate" his motivation as he goes along, if he finds or feels that he has reached a plateau. In a time of rapid industry change, intangibles like self-initiative are particularly prized—and paid for.

CHAPTER IX

A "Day" in the Life of Cheviot Securities, Inc.

We have spend a fair amount of time now on the practical details of your career search in the securities industry. Let's go back now to the framework we began with: the capital formation process. How does it work in practice? What does it accomplish for the dual interests involved: the companies and governments that are Wall Street's clients—and the securities firm that is a business in its own right? How do the two work together?

The "typical" securities company—one that does everything that the industry does, and in the same way—does not really exist. So we'll invent one. Nor can all of these activities scarcely happen in one day, so we shall move about in time to some extent. What follows, though, is not fiction. It is based on the actual experiences of managers, underwriters, salesmen, analysts, and various other securities people as they have gone about their jobs of pursuing the capital formation process from the idea stage to the investment marketplace.

Cheviot Securities, Inc., is one of the fast-rising companies in Wall Street, where it is headquartered. Founded fifty years ago by William P. Cheviot and a group of partners, the firm has seen rapid and extensive change in recent years. Cheviot himself, now well into his 70's, retired four years ago. At that time, reflecting a trend throughout Wall Street, the firm changed its form of doing business from a partnership to a corporation, with Cheviot as board chairman and 42-year-old Robert A. Taggart, who had been in charge of national retail sales, as the new president and chief executive officer.

Two years later the firm, still known as W. P. Cheviot & Co., Inc., took another big step. Again in common with many other leading firms, it went public, issuing a substantial portion of the company's stock and moving quickly to a listing on the New York Stock Exchange. Today, under its new name of Cheviot Securities, Inc., the company has a secure capital position of some $80,000,000. It operates nationwide, with some 200,000 customer accounts handled by 1,500 registered representatives at about fifty branch offices—a sales effort and organization that had been largely built under Bob Taggart's supervision. Among other new activities, Cheviot has just announced its first office overseas, in London.

This morning, as part of the preparation for Cheviot's third annual meeting of its public stockholders, Bob Taggart has been reviewing Cheviot's progress as a company—not just in the past year, but over the entire time since the firm incorporated. One of his first moves when he became chief executive was to form a Planning Department and hire a young management consultant, 33-year-old Peter Henderson, to head it. It was the first time that a formal planning function had existed at Cheviot—or, at that time, at any of the long-established securities firms.

"Where do you think we've gotten to since you arrived here, Peter?," Taggart is asking.

Henderson speaks frankly. A vice-president, he came to Cheviot on the assurance that they really wanted a planning job done, and that he would be listened to.

"I think we're making progress, but I wish it were happening faster," he says. "As you know, because I said so even before I came to the firm, I was amazed at the absolute lack of forward planning here and all over Wall Street. I think Cheviot has gotten to the point now that everyone—not just you and me—sees the need for planning. At least we've learned how much we don't know. And we can see how hard it is to predict the future of the businesses we're in. If nothing else, we've got our heads opened up to the future. We may not know yet what all the options will be. But we're in a better 'mental set' to see options when they appear, and to take advantage of them."

Three or four years ago, working with the company's other top executives, Taggart and Henderson had taken a complete inventory of Cheviot's capabilities and faults. They found that the company's main strength was in its retail sales organization, which was also backed up by a reasonably modern operations department to process orders and keep track of the firm's incoming and outgoing business. Cheviot had been operated quite conservatively down through the years, and it had a good reputation. Its customers were loyal because they knew their business was being handled responsibly.

All of this was fine—but Taggart and Henderson knew

it was not enough. Careful management had kept Cheviot out of trouble, but there were still serious flaws in the company's ways of doing business. More management reports and financial controls were needed. Cheviot's cautious course was causing it to miss business opportunities. And the firm did not know enough about its exact cost structures to realize that it might be able to do some things more aggressively, or do some other things more efficiently and use the money saved for new activities.

And new activities were badly needed. Cheviot's salesmen could effectively merchandise any securities that came along. But the firm's product line was limited—strong in the conventional common stocks, but not very sophisticated in new issues of growth companies. Cheviot was especially limited in its dealings with bonds and other fixed-income securities. And it had offered no other investment possibilities for its customers beyond stocks and bonds.

Nor was Cheviot generating much new product of its own. Its small underwriting department and syndicate staff tended to be followers rather than leaders. Cheviot was reasonably skilled in selling part of other firms' offerings, but it was seldom a major bracket or managing underwriter itself. The firm had not responded very actively to the growth of the institutional market; it did not pay enough attention to the needs of banks, insurance companies, and other large buyers of securities. The same was true of Cheviot's research department; it was small, and its security analysts served the firm's own sales staff reasonably well, but their work was not widely known or respected outside the firm by the institutions that bought research services.

Cheviot moved quickly to correct its faults over the next three years. More precise management and financial reports were begun on a daily, weekly, and monthly basis. Soon the firm began to know exactly how much it cost to do a variety of things: execute a customer's order on the floor of the New York Stock Exchange, process the securities themselves, and keep track of customer accounts, dividends, and cash balances. It learned more precisely how a salesman's time was allocated, and how much his commissions added to costs versus the firm's overall income from the business he brought in. It learned more about how to allocate clerical costs, and where automation could save the company money. It learned how much a research report cost, and how much it added to income both inside the firm and in sales to outside customers. It even found out that it was paying more to conduct some kinds of business than the business was worth in income.

Services to corporate customers were broadened by completely reorganizing the underwriting department into a new Corporate Finance Division. Besides increasing its income from underwritings and aids to corporations, Cheviot would now be able to create more products to offer all of its customers.

"We need two new departments right away," Taggart was told by Anthony Brancchia, who was hired to head the division. "We want to start a venture capital staff to be on the lookout for small, new companies as they appear and need money. Sometimes, we'll *make* them appear—start them ourselves. And we have to build an investment banking staff to handle the more mature situations—including our own ventures—when they're ready to issue stock to the public."

For the Venture Capital Department, Cheviot did what a number of firms were learning to do: it hired a venture capitalist. Gerald Warnecke had started two or three businesses of his own from scratch, building them up to a few million dollars in sales, taking them public, and then turning them over to other management or selling them to larger companies. For a while, he had headed the acquisition department of a large conglomerate, bringing in the same kinds of companies he himself had helped to start. He knew what kinds of problems a small business can face, and what kinds of people make the best founders and managers of small companies.

"Our job," he told Taggart, "is to spot a small company, look at its management and its potential marketplace, and decide if Cheviot should risk its own funds to give these guys 'seed money.' Some of these situations will grow from nothing into a prospect for our investment bankers to put together a stock issue. Other times, maybe we'll get an idea for a business ourselves, and go out to find the guys to start it. Sure, the risks are always there, and you never know. Some of these things will go over on their backs right away, some of them can be turned around again—and every once in a while we'll get a big winner for everyone concerned."

Thomas Wilson was hired by Brancchia to head the new Investment Banking Department. It was a job he had held at other firms, and he defined it this way: "We come into the process when a company has between $5,000,000 and $10,000,000 in sales and at least $500,000 in net income after taxes. But we have to see a lot more in it than that. We need an idea of how its industry is going to do for the next five years, and where this company fits in that industry. We need to know what the current market is for stocks in this kind of company. If we can't issue stock at the right time, we'll try to help in other ways. If we're convinced a company has promise, and can find a few other people that agree with us, we can do a private placement of its securities now and wait for a more receptive public market later. If a company's prospects are good, it needs money to grow right now—and the economy needs this kind of new blood down the road."

As it happens, Cheviot Securities is bringing a new issue to market this week. And it has not been an easy job. The company is Environmental Technology Corp., and it got its start three years ago when two young men—a chemical engineer and a recent M.B.A. graduate—came in to see Gerald Warnecke. Their idea was to use recent technical developments in the field of enzyme cultures to treat sewage-plant effluents and also to recycle some of the waste matter back into usable materials.

Warnecke talked with Cheviot's research specialist in pollution control and decided that there was enough to the idea to commit $200,000 of the firm's own money to the young entrepreneurs. From that "seed," Environmental Technology had grown to a $5,000,000 company. Now, it wanted additional capital to expand into chemical and petrochemical plant pollution control.

Cheviot's corporate finance staff began structuring a public issue of 200,000 shares of ETC stock. The market over the past year or so had been receptive to soundly based pollution-control stocks, and most of the companies had turned in a good record and provided their new shareholders with a good return for the investment. At first, it looked good for the ETC offering. But as the issue came due, some uncertainties developed. There was some patent trouble in the enzyme field—not directly with ETC's licenses, but in some similar techniques. The government suddenly announced some revisions in plant effluent standards. The stock market, which sometimes moves from one fad to another, became less interested in pollution control. And new issues in general were striking a softer market these days.

Two of Cheviot's people noticed the changes in the investment winds almost at the same time. Edward Marcus, the analyst that Warnecke had originally consulted, began to sense an approaching shakeout in the pollution-control industry. Inevitably, some companies were doing better than others. Some companies were having problems keeping up with this rapidly developing technology. And a more intensive government involvement was constantly changing the rules of the game.

Meanwhile, Cheviot's syndicate manager was also finding more resistance to the ETC issue than anyone had expected. Cheviot, knowing that the best deals in the world still needed skilled distribution, had upgraded its Syndicate Department at the same time it was rebuilding its corporate finance area. In a short time, 34-year-old Richard Welles had helped bring the firm into a leading position as a managing underwriter and a sought-after major bracket participant in other firms' new issues.

Welles had been carefully building the selling group for ETC's stock over a period of several weeks. He first invited the dozen or so other firms that he thought were the best candidates to take a major portion of the ETC issue: firms with a known ability to distribute stock responsibly and effectively. While they considered the deal, Welles made a broad mailing to about 300 other firms that at one time or another had been in on Cheviot's issues. As expressions of interest came in from both the major bracket firms and the smaller companies, Welles continued to refine the list to assure ETC of a broad geographical distribution of its stock—and to make sure the stock was going to firms that could sell as much as they promised.

"You take from the weak and give to the strong," was Welles's favorite way of putting it. "We have to watch out for brokers who will take any stock whether they know their customers will be interested or not. Or worse, they'll sell their stock back into the market the same day —taking advantage of a quick price rise for themselves, but depressing the price for long-term investors."

A week or so ago, Welles had had his selling group pretty well buttoned up. Now, some members were "uncircling"—reducing the number of shares they wanted, or canceling out entirely. All of this was perfectly fair practice before a new issue came out, but it was bad news for the underwriter and his client.

The afternoon before the issue, Cheviot's executives sat down with the founders of ETC to decide whether or not to go ahead and, if they did go ahead, to set the final price of the stock. There was talk of postponing the issue until some of the questions were cleared up and there was a better market. But both ETC and its underwriters still believed the company's record would stand up with investors, and that this was the time to find out. The decision was to bring the deal to the market.

Cheviot had one suggestion. "Our role is the middleman," said Welles. "We try to find a fair price for both the seller and the buyer. I think ETC stands a better chance of a successful long-term issue if we price the stock at $12.50 a share instead of the $15 we had hoped for at first. You'll raise $2,500,000 instead of $3,000,000, but you'll get a better shareholder base now and probably a more receptive market for future offerings." The company agreed with this reasoning, and so did Cheviot's own corporate finance staff, even though the change meant a reduction in their underwriting fee. Cheviot had been in on ETC's growth from the start, and both companies valued the long relationship and their mutual interest in the future over any maximum short-run gains.

The day that ETC's stock came to market, Cheviot's sales staff confirmed the wisdom of the decision to bring the company out right away at a lower price. Jonathan Henseagull, a registered representative in the firm's Philadelphia branch, had been following pollution-control stocks with interest since he had finished his nine-month training program the year before. He was interested in environmental subjects, and his location in a large metropolitan area with extensive waterways and a concentration of chemical plants gave him a close view of pollution problems and the public's attitude about them. He had also talked to many of his good customers about pollution-control stocks as an investment—putting their money to work to upgrade the environment. He found them very receptive to the new stock—particularly when it came at a better price than expected. And the same turned out to be true with salesmen throughout Cheviot's nationwide syndicate.

In Cheviot's research department, analyst Edward Misfit was pleased with the issue for two reasons. He had been worried that the recent uncertainties in the pollution-control field were having negative effects on the entire industry—including the quality companies like Environmental Technology. But he was also happy with the role he himself had had in ETC's development from the start. Not long out of college, with a degree in economics, Misfit had set his sights on security analysis as a career—working first at a bank, then with a mutual fund group, and finally on Wall Street. Besides putting himself through the Chartered Financial Analysts program, he had gone back to college for courses in accounting, law, and chemistry—and he felt his efforts were paying off.

Too often, Misfit felt, the analyst's role was confined to securities after they had come all the way through the capital formation process. With ETC, he had been in on Cheviot's dealings with the client from the time the technology company was first formed all the way through to its first public issue. And he would continue to follow the company, for Cheviot and other firms, as it grew even further.

So ETC's stock issue, despite last-minute worries, seemed to be a success—for everyone. A few days later, Bob Taggart and Peter Henderson were talking about it.

"That one had me worried," Taggart confessed. "We've come too far to be overturned by a bad new issue market or some government regulations no one has figured out yet."

Henderson, as usual, was quick to jump on his boss's words. "That's just the point, though," he said. "We all worked together to bring Environmental Technology on the market, and we've gotten to the point where we do that better than most firms do. But we haven't come far enough if we *can* be upset by one bad market or a new policy out of Washington. That kind of thing is going to happen in this industry all the time, and probably more often in the future."

Taggart was amused, but he knew Henderson was right. "I don't need to ask," he said, "but where do you think we can do better?"

Henderson opened a folder he was carrying. "Okay, here's where we went wrong," he said. "Our research was good—but we still should have had an earlier warning than we did. Corporate Finance should have had five other ways ready to help that company raise money if it couldn't issue stock right now. Syndicate shouldn't have to wait until the last minute to reset the price. And we didn't pay close enough attention to the institutional interest in these stocks. Beyond all that, we shouldn't be so dependent on the stock market all the time. Our customers deserve more to choose from. If we don't provide it, someone else will. If the sales staff meets resistance to securities, we need to give them other products and services to sell. We need more services for corporations, too. The society is demanding more, and that's going to change this business. We're not changing fast enough with it. This company has got to get its head out of today! Now, here are some ideas . . ."

CHAPTER X

Tomorrow's Securities Industry

"The future lies ahead," said comedian Mort Sahl. Brief as it is, the quip covers a wide range of today's uncertainties—sometimes, it seems that this is all we can say for an absolute certainty. Peter Henderson at Cheviot Securities was saying the same thing to Bob Taggart. And this book about careers in the securities industry is saying the same thing to you.

It would be foolish for a book about careers in any field to do otherwise. A book about space technology, written in 1957 before the first Russian Sputnik, could only have discussed interplanetary travel in the most tentative way; fewer than fifteen years later, a dozen Americans had walked, driven, and played golf on the moon. A book about medicine, ten years ago, would have been very theoretical about heart transplants. How many people in the automotive field, five years ago, knew much about Wankel engines?

So is the securities industry changing, even as this book is written. That does not mean you have wasted your time with the last nine chapters. Change is sweeping broadly through Wall Street, as any current issue of *The Wall Street Journal* or *Business Week* will tell you. But the same publications, and many others in the business field, will document that the same process of change is abroad in all of the financial industries—in all of business. The times demand it, and on a worldwide basis.

The financial industries—securities included—are in the forefront of change precisely because they hold the central role in society that we have tried to make the theme of this book. One Wall Street broker was talking recently about his favorite subject—banking—but he might have meant the securities business as well. "I don't know of any other industry that is as fully insulated from obsolescence," he said. "The Phoenicians needed money, and *we* need money."

But change, except in the very worst of times, is evolutionary. It does not happen overnight, generally—nor should it. You will find, even if you enter a securities career tomorrow morning, that changes are taking place and being talked about all around you. But you will also find that much of what we have described is essentially the same as you have found it here. And whatever is new, you will see, is only adding to the future excitement and usefulness of careers in this business.

We have already mentioned in passing a good many of the things that are going on in the securities industry right now. Companies are diversifying into broader lines of financial services. Automation is more widespread all the time. There is more emphasis on a deeper sophistication of management, and on planning. The marketplaces are becoming more efficient. And—possibly the most exciting of all—there is the internationalization of the financial world, and the securities industry with it.

We were reasonably able to construct a profile of Cheviot Securities, Inc., as such a firm might exist today. But it would be as difficult to project what Cheviot might look like in the 1980's as it would have been to describe accurately an extravehicular space walk in 1957. We can, though, take a stab at some of its characteristics.

Very likely, if present trends continue, Cheviot and a good number of similar firms will have changed themselves into holding companies long before 1980. This will mean that the parent organization will operate any number of separate subsidiaries in various financial fields and perhaps some other, less closely related, areas. Much of the securities business will be just one subsidiary. Others might be in insurance, commodities, mortgage banking, savings and loan activities, publishing, or accounting. That may sound like a mixed bag of businesses—but a common thread of money and information passes through all of them, and the two are very necessary to each other. "More and more, we are all in the information business," says one Wall Street security analyst.

The financial flexibility of a holding company structure has a good deal of appeal to a number of security companies, as the industry's own capital needs are growing apace with the world that the industry provides with capital. For that matter, we need not conjecture about the holding company plans of our fictional Cheviot Securities: In 1973 at least four of its major real-life counterparts—Merrill Lynch; E. F. Hutton; Paine, Webber, Jackson & Curtis; and Donaldson, Lufkin & Jenrette—

all have already gotten their shareholders' approval to form holding companies.

As securities companies broaden and grow, so do their marketplaces. The New York Stock Exchange today differs greatly from the Exchange of ten years ago—let alone from its profile at the turn of the century or back in the days of small gatherings under the buttonwood tree. Increasingly computerized, a corporation in its own right, the Exchange intends to be the cornerstone of the future's central financial marketplace, sharing services and information with other exchanges around the United States—and, one likely day, around the world.

The mounting multinationality of all business activity is taking place so fast that it is scarcely possible for an observer to keep up with it. It is not at all unlikely that, by the end of the 1970's, the financial dimensions of American capital markets will be challenged in a significant way on one side of the world by those of the European Common Market, and on the other side of the world by an Asian capital market stretching from Tokyo to Hong Kong and Singapore. Corporate and government financings are already taking place between institutions of many nations, including consortia of banks and investment houses that bring the interests of the United States, Great Britain, Germany, Norway, Switzerland, and Japan into the same transactions. Individual securities trade now across the borders and oceans between European countries, Latin America, the United States, and the Far East.

Already today, more than 300 offices of New York

Stock Exchange member firms are located all around the world to handle multinational activities in everything from securities and commodities to investment banking. And the trend is multilateral: One of the leading Japanese securities firms celebrated in mid-1973 the twentieth anniversary of its New York office; its counterparts from Europe have been here as long or longer. The "tombstone" ads of investment syndicates in the United States today are increasingly populated, in higher and higher positions, with the names of leading investment houses from all over the world.

Some thirty years ago, at the awful height of World War II, Wendell L. Willkie returned from a 31,000-mile trip through the chaos to write *One World*—a book that turned out to be a prescient blueprint for much of the economic cooperation and communal multinational interests that are maturing only today. Willkie was a visionary businessman who knew the way that the world one day must work.

His vision was hard to accept then, and proved even harder to implement when peace as we have known it came a few years later. But today, almost two generations later, Willkie's *One World* seems at last upon us, and the securities industry is very much a part of it. Wendell Willkie had his head very much out of the "today" of that unlikely year of 1943, and very much into his future, our present. Today, if you can say the same, *your* future in securities offers you opportunities to participate and contribute in ways that your predecessors—those who made this book for you—were seldom able to dream of.

APPENDIX I

New York Stock Exchange Regional Firms

Robert W. Baird & Co., Incorporated
731 North Water Street, Milwaukee, Wisconsin 53202
Bateman Eichler, Hill Richards, Incorporated
460 South Spring Street, Los Angeles, California 90014
A. G. Becker & Co. Incorporated
Two First National Plaza, Chicago, Illinois 60670
Boettcher and Company
828 17th Street, Denver, Colorado 80202
Alex Brown & Sons
135 East Baltimore Street, Baltimore, Maryland 21202
Cantella & Co.
225 Franklin Street, Boston, Massachusetts 02110
Dain, Kalman & Quail, Incorporated
100 Dain Tower, Minneapolis, Minnesota 55402
A. G. Edwards & Sons, Inc.
One North Jefferson Street, St. Louis, Missouri 63103
J. J. B. Hilliard, W. L. Lyons, Inc.
545 South Third Street, Louisville, Kentucky 40202
Janney Montgomery Scott Inc.
1401 Walnut Street, Philadelphia, Pennsylvania 19102
Loewi & Co. Incorporated
225 East Mason Street, Milwaukee, Wisconsin 53202
McDonald & Company
2100 Central National Bank Building, Cleveland, Ohio 44114
Prescott, Ball & Turben
900 National City Bank Building, Cleveland, Ohio, 44114
Rauscher Pierce Securities Corporation
1200 Mercantile Dallas Building, Dallas, Texas 75201

The Robinson-Humphrey Company, Inc.
Two Peachtree Street, N.W., Atlanta, Georgia 30303
Rotan Mosle Inc.
2200 Bank of the Southwest Building, Houston, Texas 77002
Stifel, Nicolaus & Company Incorporated
314 North Broadway, St. Louis, Missouri 63102
Sutro & Co. Incorporated
460 Montgomery Street, San Francisco, California 94104
Wheat, First Securities, Inc.
801 East Main Street, Richmond, Virginia 23211

APPENDIX II

Thirty Major

New York Stock Exchange Firms

Bache & Co. Incorporated
100 Gold Street, New York, New York 10038
Baker, Weeks & Co., Inc.
One Battery Park Plaza, New York, New York 10004
Bear, Stearns & Co.
One Wall Street, New York, New York 10005
A. G. Becker & Co. Incorporated
Two First National Plaza, Chicago, Illinois 60670
Blyth Eastman Dillon & Co. Incorporated
One Chase Manhattan Plaza, New York, New York 10005
Clark, Dodge & Co. Incorporated
140 Broadway, New York, New York 10005
Drexel, Burnham & Co. Inc.
60 Broad Street, New York, New York 10005
duPont Glore Forgan Incorporated
1 Wall Street, New York, New York 10005
duPont Walston Incorporated
77 Water Street, New York, New York
Goldman, Sachs & Co.
55 Broad Street, New York, New York 10004
Harris, Upham & Co. Incorporated
120 Broadway, New York, New York 10005
Hornblower & Weeks-Hemphill, Noyes Incorporated
8 Hanover Square, New York, New York 10004
E. F. Hutton & Company Inc.
One Battery Park Plaza, New York, New York 10004

W. E. Hutton & Company
14 Wall Street, New York, New York 10005
Kidder, Peabody & Co. Incorporated
10 Hanover Square, New York, New York 10005
Lehman Brothers Incorporated
One William Street, New York, New York 10004
Loeb, Rhoades & Co.
42 Wall Street, New York, New York 10005
Merrill Lynch, Pierce, Fenner & Smith Incorporated
One Liberty Plaza, New York, New York 10006
Oppenheimer & Co.
One New York Plaza, New York, New York 10004
Paine, Webber, Jackson & Curtis Incorporated
140 Broadway, New York, New York 10005
Pershing & Co. Inc.
120 Broadway, New York, New York 10005
Reynolds Securities Inc.
120 Broadway, New York, New York 10005
Salomon Brothers
One New York Plaza, New York, New York 10004
Shearson, Hammill & Co. Incorporated
14 Wall Street, New York, New York 10005
Shields & Co. Incorporated
44 Wall Street, New York, New York 10005
Smith, Barney & Co. Incorporated
1345 Avenue of the Americas, New York, New York 10019
Thomson & McKinnon Auchincloss Inc.
Two Broadway, New York, New York 10004
Spencer Trask & Co. Incorporated
60 Broad Street, New York, New York 10004
White, Weld & Co. Incorporated
One Liberty Plaza, New York, New York 10005
Dean Witter & Co. Incorporated
45 Montgomery Street, San Francisco, California 94106

Glossary

Glossary material
supplied courtesy of
the New York Stock Exchange.

Annual Report The formal financial statement issued yearly by a corporation to its shareowners. The annual report shows assets, liabilities, earnings—how the company stood at the close of the business year and how it fared profitwise during the year.

Arbitrage A technique employed to take advantage of differences in price. If, for example, XYZ stock can be bought in New York for $10 a share and sold in London at $10.50, an arbitrageur may simultaneously purchase XYZ stock here and sell the same amount in London, making a profit of 50 cents a share, less expenses. Arbitrage may also involve the purchase of rights to subscribe to a security, or the purchase of a convertible security—and the sale at or about the same time of the security obtainable through exercise of the rights or of the security obtainable through conversion. (See: *Convertible; Rights*)

Assets Everything a corporation owns or is due to it: cash, investments, money due it, materials and inventories, which are called current assets; buildings and machinery, which are known as fixed assets; and patents and good-will, called intangible assets. (See: *Liabilities*)

Averages Various ways of measuring the trend of securities prices, the most popular of which is the Dow-Jones average of 30 industrial stocks listed on the New York Stock Exchange. The term average has led to considerable confusion. A simple average for, say, 50 leading stocks would be obtained by totaling the prices of all and dividing by 50. But suppose one of the stocks in the average is split. The price of each share of that stock is then automatically reduced because more shares are outstanding. Thus the average would decline even if all other issues in the average were unchanged. That average thus becomes inaccurate as an indicator of the market's trend.

Various formulas—some very elaborate—have been devised to compensate for stock splits and stock dividends and thus give continuity to the average. Averages and individual stock prices belong in separate compartments.

In the case of the Dow-Jones industrial average, the prices of the 30 stocks are totaled and then divided by a divisor which is intended to compensate for past stock splits and dividends and which is changed from time to time. As a result point changes in the average have only the vaguest relationship to dollar price changes in stocks included in the average. In November, 1968, the divisor was 2.011, so that a one-point change in the industrial average at that time was actually the equivalent of 6.7 cents. (See: *NYSE Common Stock Index; Point; Split*)

Averaging (See: *Dollar Cost Averaging*)

Balance Sheet A condensed statement showing the nature and amount of a company's assets, liabilities, and capital on a given date. In dollar amounts the balance sheet shows what the company owned, what it owed, and the ownership interest in the company of its stockholders. (See: *Assets; Earnings Report*)

Bear Someone who believes the market will decline. (See: *Bull*)

Bear Market A declining market. (See: *Bull Market*)

Bearer Bond A bond which does not have the owner's name registered on the books of the issuing company and which is payable to the holder. (See: *Coupon Bond; Registered Bond*)

Bid and Asked Often referred to as a quotation or quote. The bid is the highest price anyone has declared that he wants to pay for a security at a given time; the asked is the lowest price anyone will take at the same time. (See: *Quotation*)

Big Board A popular term for the New York Stock Exchange.

Blue Chip Common stock in a company known nationally for the quality and wide acceptance of its products or services, and for its ability to make money and pay dividends. Usually such stocks are relatively high priced and offer relatively low yields.

Blue Sky Laws A popular name for laws various states have enacted to protect the public against securities frauds. The term is believed to have originated when a judge ruled that a particular stock had about the same value as a patch of blue sky.

Board Room A room for customers in a broker's office where opening, high, low, and last prices of leading stocks are posted on a board throughout the market day.

Boiler Room Operation High-pressure peddling over the telephone of stocks of dubious value. A typical boiler room is simply a room lined with desks or cubicles, each with a salesman and telephone. The salesmen call persons on what are known in the trade as sucker lists.

Bond Basically an IOU or promissory note of a corporation, usually issued in multiples of $1,000, although $100 and $500 denominations are not uncommon. A bond is evidence of a debt on which the issuing company usually promises to pay the bondholders a specified amount of interest for a specified length of time, and to repay the loan on the expiration date. In every case a bond represents debt—its holder is a creditor of the corporation and not a part owner as is the shareholder. (See: *Collateral Trust Bond; Convertible; General Mortgage Bond; Income Bond*)

Book A notebook the specialist in a stock uses to keep a record of the buy and sell orders at specified prices, in sequence of receipt, which are left with him by other brokers. (See: *Specialist*)

Book Value An accounting term. Book value of a stock is determined from a company's records, by adding all assets (generally excluding such intangibles as goodwill), then deducting all debts and other liabilities, plus the liquidation price of any preferred issues. The sum arrived at is divided by the number of common shares outstanding, and the result is book value per common share. Book value of the assets of a company or a security may have little or no significant relationship to market value.

Broker An agent, often a member of a stock exchange firm or an exchange member himself, who handles the public's orders to buy and sell securities or commodities. For this service a commission is charged. (See: *Commission Broker; Dealer*)

Brokers' Loans Money borrowed by brokers from banks for a variety of uses. It may be used by specialists and odd-lot dealers to help finance inventories of stocks they deal in; by brokerage firms to finance the underwriting of new issues of corporate and municipal securities; to help finance a firm's own investments; and to help finance the purchase of securities for customers who prefer to use the broker's credit when they buy securities. (See: *Call Loan; Margin*)

Bucket Shop An illegal operation now almost extinct. The bucket-shop operator accepted a client's money without ever actually buying or selling securities as the client ordered. Instead he held the money and gambled that the customer was wrong. When too many customers were right, the bucket shop closed its doors and opened a new office.

Bull One who believes the market will rise. (See: *Bear*)

Bull Market An advancing market. (See: *Bear Market*)

Call Loan A loan that may be terminated or "called" at any time by the lender or borrower. Used to finance purchases of securities. (See: *Brokers' Loans*)

Calls (See: *Puts and Calls*)

Capital Gain or Capital Loss Profit or loss from the sale of a capital asset. A capital gain, under current Federal income tax laws, may be either short-term (6 months or less) or long-term (more than 6 months). A short-term capital gain is taxed at the reporting individual's full income tax rate. A long-term capital gain up to $50,000 ($25,000 in the case of a married individual filing a separate return) is normally taxed at a maximum of 25 percent, depending on the reporting individual's tax bracket. Up to $1,000 ($500 in the case of a married individual filing a separate return) of net capital loss (that is, when you sell securities at a lower price than you paid for them) is deductible from the individual's taxable income during the year reported. If the net capital loss is a long-term capital loss, a deduction is allowed for only one-half of the net capital loss up to the maximum amount of $1,000. If the net capital loss is more than $1,000 in any one year (or $2,000 if the net capital loss is a long-term capital loss), as much as $1,000 annually may be deducted in future years until the amount deductible as a loss has been utilized. The amount of the net capital loss which may be deducted in future years is reduced by the amount of capital gain in such years.

Capital Stock All shares representing ownership of a business, including preferred and common. (See: *Common Stock; Preferred Stock*)

Capitalization Total amount of the various securities issued by a corporation. Capitalization may include bonds, debentures, preferred and common stock, and surplus. Bonds and debentures are usually carried on the books of the issuing company in terms of their par or face value. Preferred and common shares may be carried in terms of par or stated value. Stated value may be an arbitrary figure decided upon by the directors or may represent the amount received by the company from the sale of the securities at the time of issuance. (See: *Par*)

Cash Flow Reported net income of a corporation *plus* amounts charged off for depreciation, depletion, amortization, extraordinary charges to reserves, which are bookkeeping deductions and not paid out in actual dollars and cents. (See: *Depletion; Depreciation*)

Cash Sale A transaction on the floor of the Stock Exchange calls for delivery of the securities the same day. In "regular way" trades, the seller is to deliver on the fifth business day.

Certificate The actual piece of paper that is evidence of ownership of stock in a corporation. Watermarked paper is finely engraved with delicate etchings to discourage forgery. Loss of a certificate may at the least cause a great deal of inconvenience—at the worst, financial loss.

Central Certificate Service (CCS) A department of Stock Clearing Corporation which conducts a central securities certificate operation through which clearing firms effect security deliveries between each other via computerized bookkeeping entries, thereby reducing the physical movement of stock certificates. (See: *Stock Clearing Corporation*)

Closed-End Investment Trust (See: *Investment Trust*)

Collateral Securities or other property pledged by a borrower to secure repayment of a loan.

Collateral Trust Bond A bond secured by collateral deposited with a trustee. The collateral is often the stocks or bonds of companies controlled by the issuing company but may be other securities.

Commission The broker's basic fee for purchasing or selling securities or property as an agent. The New York Stock Exchange fixes minimum commission rates applicable to orders to purchase or sell NYSE listed stocks involving $500,000 or less. Commissions on portions of orders in excess of $500,000 are subject to negotiation.

Commission Broker An agent who executes the public's orders for the purchase or sale of securities or commodities. (See: *Broker; Dealer*)

Common Stock Securities that represent an ownership interest in a corporation. If the company has also issued preferred stock, both common and preferred have ownership rights, but the preferred normally has prior claim on dividends and, in the event of liquidation, assets. Claims of both common and preferred stockholders are junior to claims of bondholders or other creditors of the company. Common stockholders assume the greater risk, but generally exercise the greater control and may gain the greater reward in the form of dividends and capital appreciation. The terms common stock and capital stock are often used interchangeably when the company has no preferred stock. (See: *Capital Stock; Preferred Stock*)

Conglomerate A corporation seeking to diversify its operations by acquiring enterprises in widely varied industries.

Consolidated Balance Sheet A balance sheet showing the financial condition of a corporation and its subsidiaries. (See: *Balance Sheet*)

Convertible A bond, debenture, or preferred share which may be exchanged by the owner for common stock or another security, usually of the same company, in accordance with the terms of the issue.

Corner Buying of a stock or commodity on a scale large enough to give the buyer, or buying group, control over the price. A person who must buy that stock or commodity, for example one who is short, is forced to do business at an arbitrarily high price with those who obtained the corner. (See: *Short Position; Short Sale*)

Correspondent A securities firm, bank, or other financial organization that regularly performs services for another in a place or market to which the other does not have direct access. Securities firms may have correspondents in foreign countries or on exchanges of which they are not members. Correspondents are frequently linked by private wires. Member organizations of the NYSE with offices in New York City also act as correspondents for out-of-town member organizations that do not maintain New York City offices.

Coupon Bond Bond with interest coupons attached. The coupons are clipped as they came due and are presented by the holder for payment of interest. (See: *Bearer Bond, Registered Bond*)

Covering Buying a security previously sold short. (See: *Short Sale*)

Cumulative Preferred A stock having a provision that if one or more dividends are omitted, the omitted dividends must be paid before dividends may be paid on the company's common stock.

Cumulative Voting A method of voting for corporate directors which enables the shareholder to multiply the number of his shares by the number of directorships being voted on and cast the total for one director or a selected group of directors. A 10-share holder normally casts 10 votes for each of, say 12 nominees to the board of directors. He thus has 120 votes. Under the cumulative voting principle he may do that or he may cast 120 (10x12) votes for only one nominee, 60 for two, 40 for three, or any other distribution he chooses. Cumulative voting is required under the corporate laws of some states, is permitted in most others.

Curb Exchange Former name of the American Stock Exchange, second largest exchange in the country. The term comes from the market's origin on a street in downtown New York.

Current Assets Those assets of a company which are reasonably expected to be realized in cash, or sold, or consumed during the normal operating cycle of the business. These include cash, U.S. Government bonds, receivables and money due usually within one year, and inventories.

Current Liabilities Money owed and payable by a company, usually within one year.

Current Return (See: *Yield*)

Customers' Man (See: *Registered Representative*)

Customers' Net Debit Balances Credit of New York Stock Exchange member firms made available to help finance customers' purchases of stocks, bonds, and commodities.

Dealer An individual or firm in the securities business acting as a principal rather than as an agent. Typically, a dealer buys for his own account and sells to a customer from his own inventory. The dealer's profit or loss is the difference between the price he pays and the price he receives for the same security. The dealer's confirmation must disclose to his customer that he has acted as principal. The same individual or firm may function, at different times, either as broker or dealer. (See: *NASD; Specialist*)

Debenture A promissory note backed by the general credit of a company and usually not secured by a mortgage or lien on any specific property. (See: *Bond*)

Depletion Natural resources, such as metals, oils and gas, timber, which conceivably can be reduced to zero over the years, present a special problem in capital management. Depletion is an accounting practice consisting of charges against earnings based upon the amount of the asset taken out of the total reserves in the period for which accounting is made. A bookkeeping entry, it does not represent any cash outlay, nor are any funds earmarked for the purpose.

Depreciation Normally, charges against earnings to write off the cost, less salvage value, of an asset over its estimated useful life. It is a bookkeeping entry, and does not represent any cash outlay, nor are any funds earmarked for the purpose.

Director Person elected by shareholders to establish company policies. The directors appoint the president, vice-presidents, and all other operating officers. Directors decide, among other matters, if and when dividends shall be paid. (See: *Management; Proxy*)

Discretionary Account An account in which the customer gives the broker or someone else discretion, which may be complete or within specific limits, as to the purchase and sale of securities or commodities, including selection, timing, amount, and price to be paid or received.

Discretionary Order The customer empowers the broker to act on his behalf with respect to the choice of security to be bought or sold, a total amount of any securities to be bought or sold, and/or whether any such transaction shall be one of purchase or sale.

Diversification Spreading investments among different companies in different fields. Another type of diversification is also offered by the securities of many individual companies because of the wide range of their activities. (See: *Investment Trust*)

Dividend The payment designated by the Board of Directors to be distributed pro rata among the shares outstanding. On preferred shares, it is generally a fixed amount. On common shares, the dividend varies with the fortunes of the company and the amount of cash on hand, and may be omitted if business is poor or the directors determine to withhold earnings to invest in plant and equipment. Sometimes a company will pay a dividend out of past earnings even if it is not currently operating at a profit.

Dollar Cost Averaging A system of buying securities at regular intervals with a fixed dollar amount. Under this system the investor buys by the dollars' worth rather than by the number of shares. If each investment is of the same number of dollars, payments buy more when the price is low and fewer when it rises. Thus temporary downswings in price benefit the investor if he continues periodic purchases in both good times and bad and the price at which the shares are sold is more than their average cost. (See: *Formula Investing*)

Double Taxation Short for Double Taxation of Dividends. The federal government taxes corporate profits once as corporate income; any part of the remaining profits distributed as dividends to stockholders is taxed again as income to the recipient stockholder.

Dow Theory A theory of market analysis based upon the performance of the Dow-Jones industrial and rail stock price averages. The theory says that the market is in a basic upward trend if one of these averages advances above a previous important high, accompanied or followed by a similar advance in the other. When the averages both dip below previous important lows, this is regarded as confirmation of a basic downward trend. The theory does not attempt to predict how long either trend will continue, although it is widely misinterpreted as a method of forecasting future action. Whatever the merits of the theory, it is sometimes a strong factor in the market because many people believe in the theory—or believe that a great many others do. (See: *Technical Position*)

Down Tick (See: *Up Tick*)

Earnings Report A statement—also called an income statement —issued by a company showing its earnings or losses over a given period. The earnings report lists the income earned, expenses, and the net result. (See: *Balance Sheet*)

Equipment Trust Certificate A type of security, generally issued by a railroad, to pay for new equipment. Title to the equipment, such as a locomotive, is held by a trustee until the notes are paid off. An equipment trust certificate is usually secured by a first claim on the equipment.

Equity The ownership interest of common and preferred stockholders in a company. Also refers to excess of value of securities over the debit balance in a margin account.

Exchange Acquisition A method of filling an order to buy a large block of stock on the floor of the Exchange. Under certain circumstances, a member-broker can facilitate the purchase of a block by soliciting orders to sell. All orders to sell the security are lumped together and crossed with the buy order in the regular auction market. The price to the buyer may be on a net basis or on a commission basis.

Exchange Distribution A method of disposing of large blocks of stock on the floor of the Exchange. Under certain circumstances, a member-broker can facilitate the sale of a block of stock by soliciting and getting other member-brokers to solicit orders to buy. Individual buy orders are lumped together and crossed with the sell order in the regular auction market. A special commission is usually paid by the seller; ordinarily the buyer pays no commission.

Ex-Dividend A synonym for "without dividend." The buyer of a stock selling ex-dividend does not receive the recently declared dividend. Open buy and sell stop orders, and sell stop limit orders in a stock on the ex-dividend date are ordinarily reduced by the value of that dividend. In the case of open stop limit orders to sell, both the stop price and the limit price are reduced. Every dividend is payable on a fixed date to all shareholders recorded on the books of the company as of a previous date of record. For example, a dividend may be declared as payable to holders of record on the books of the company on a given Friday. Since five business days are allowed for delivery of stock in a "regular way" transaction on the New York Stock Exchange, the Exchange would declare the stock "ex-dividend" as of the opening of the market on the preceding Monday. That means anyone who bought it on and after Monday would not be entitled to that dividend. (See: *Cash Sale; Net Change; Transfer*)

Ex-Rights Without the rights. Corporations raising additional money may do so by offering their stockholders the right to subscribe to new or additional stock, usually at a discount from the prevailing market price. The buyer of a stock selling ex-rights is not entitled to the rights. (See: *Ex-Dividend; Rights*)

Extra The short form of "extra dividend." A dividend in the form of stock or cash in addition to the regular or usual dividend the company has been paying.

Face Value The value of a bond that appears on the face of the bond, unless the value is otherwise specified by the issuing company. Face value is ordinarily the amount the issuing company promises to pay at maturity. Face value in not an indication of market value. Sometimes referred to as par value. (See: *Par*)

Fiscal Year A corporation's accounting year. Due to the nature of their particular business, some companies do not use the calendar year for their bookkeeping. A typical example is the department store which finds December 31 too early a date to close its books after the Christmas rush. For that reason many stores wind up their accounting year January 31. Their fiscal year, therefore, runs from February 1 of one year through January 31 of the next. The fiscal year of other companies may run from July 1 through the following June 30. Most companies, though, operate on a calendar-year basis.

Fixed Charges A company's fixed expenses, such as bond interest, which it has agreed to pay whether or not earned, and which are deducted from income before earnings on equity capital are computed.

Flat This term means that the price at which a bond is traded includes consideration for all unpaid accruals of interest. Bonds which are in default of interest or principal are traded flat. Income bonds, which pay interest only to the extent earned are usually traded flat. All other bonds are usually dealt in "and interest," which means that the buyer pays to the seller the market price plus interest accrued since the last payment date. When applied to a stock loan, flat means without premium or interest. (See: *Short Sale*)

Floor The huge trading area—about two thirds the size of a football field—where stocks and bonds are bought and sold on the New York Stock Exchange.

Floor Broker A member of a stock exchange who executes orders on the floor of the exchange to buy or sell any listed securities. (See: *Commission Broker; Two-Dollar Broker*)

Floor Trader (See: *Registered Trader*)

Fluctuation (See: *Point*)

Formula Investing Investment techniques. One formula calls for the shifting of funds from common shares to preferred shares or bonds as the market, on average, rises above a certain predetermined point—and the return of funds to common share investments as the market average declines. (See: *Dollar Cost Averaging*)

Free and Open Market A market in which supply and demand are expressed in terms of price. Contrasts with a controlled market in which supply, demand, and price may all be regulated.

Funded Debt Usually interest-bearing bonds or debentures of a company. May include long-term bank loans. Does *not* include short-term loans, preferred or common stock.

General Mortgage Bond A bond that is secured by a blanket mortgage on the company's property, but is often outranked by one or more other mortgages.

Gilt-Edged Bond High-grade bond issued by a company which has demonstrated its ability to earn a comfortable profit over a period of years and pay its bondholders their interest without interruption.

Give Up A term with many different meanings. For one, a member of the Exchange on the floor may act for a second member by executing an order for him with a third member. The first member tells the third member that he is acting on behalf of the second member and "gives up" the second member's name rather than his own. For another, if you have an account with Doe & Company but you're in a town where Doe has no office, you go to another member firm, tell them you have an account with Doe & Company and would like to buy some stock. After verifying your account with Doe & Company, the firm may execute your order and tell the broker who sells the stock that the firm is acting on behalf of Doe & Company. They give up the name of Doe & Company to the selling broker. Or the firm may simply wire your order to Doe & Company who will execute it for you. The term "give up" has also been applied to a variety of other arrangements, most of which are no longer permitted.

Good Delivery Certain basic qualifications must be met before a security sold on the Exchange may be delivered. The security must be in proper form to comply with the contract of sale and to transfer title to the purchaser.

Government Bonds Obligations of the U.S. Government, regarded as the highest-grade issues in existence.

Growth Stock Stock of a company with prospects for future growth—a company whose earnings are expected to increase at a relatively rapid rate.

Guaranteed Bond A bond which has interest or principal, or both, guaranteed by a company other than the issuer. Usually found in the railroad industry when large roads, leasing sections of trackage owned by small railroads, may guarantee the bonds of the smaller road.

Guaranteed Stock Usually preferred stock on which dividends are guaranteed by another company, under much the same circumstances as a bond is guaranteed.

Hedge (See: *Arbitrage; Puts & Calls; Selling Short Against the Box; Short Sale*)

Holding Company A corporation which owns the securities of another, in most cases with voting control.

Hypothecation The pledging of securities as collateral for a loan.

Inactive Post A trading post on the floor of the New York Stock Exchange where inactive securities are traded in units of 10 shares instead of the usual 100-share lots. Better known in the business as Post 30. (See: *Round Lot*)

Inactive Stock An issue traded on an exchange or in the over-the-counter market in which there is a relatively low volume of transactions. Volume may be no more than a few hundred shares a week or even less. On the New York Stock Exchange many inactive stocks are traded in 10-share units rather than the customary 100. (See: *Round Lot*)

In-and-Out Purchase and sale of the same security within a short period—a day, week, even a month. An in-and-out trader is generally more interested in day-to-day price fluctuations than dividends or long-term growth.

Income Bond Generally, income bonds promise to repay principal but to pay interest only when earned. In some cases unpaid interest on an income bond may accumulate as a claim against the corporation when the bond becomes due. An income bond may also be issued in lieu of preferred stock.

Indenture A written agreement under which debentures are issued, setting forth maturity date, interest rate, and other terms.

Index A statistical yardstick expressed in terms of percentages of a base year or years. For instance, the Federal Reserve Board's index of industrial production is based on 1957–59 as 100. In

January, 1971, the index stood at 165.1, which meant that industrial production that month was about 65 percent higher than in the base period. An index is not an average. (See: *Averages; NYSE Common Stock Index*)

Interest Payments a borrower pays a lender for the use of his money. A corporation pays interest on its bonds to its bondholders. (See: *Bond; Dividend*)

Investment The use of money for the purpose of making more money, to gain income, or increase capital, or both. Safety of principal is an important consideration. (See: *Speculation*)

Investment Banker Also known as an underwriter. He is the middleman between the corporation issuing new securities and the public. The usual practice is for one or more investment bankers to buy outright from a corporation a new issue of stocks or bonds. The group forms a syndicate to sell the securities to individuals and institutions. Investment bankers also distribute very large blocks of stocks or bonds—perhaps held by an estate. Thereafter the market in the security may be over-the-counter, on a regional stock exchange, the American Exchange, or the New York Stock Exchange. (See: *Over-the-Counter; Primary Distribution; Syndicate*)

Investment Counsel One whose principal business consists of acting as investment adviser and a substantial part of whose business consists of rendering investment supervisory services.

Investment Trust A company or trust that uses its capital to invest in other companies. There are two principal types: the closed-end and the open-end, or mutual fund. Shares in closed-end investment trusts, some of which are listed on the New York Stock Exchange, are readily transferable in the open market and are bought and sold like other shares. Capitalization of these companies remains the same unless action is taken to change, which is seldom. Open-end funds sell their own new shares to investors, stand ready to buy back their old shares, and are not listed. Open-end funds are so called because their capitalization is not fixed; they issue more shares as people want them.

Investor An individual whose principal concerns in the purchase of a security are regular dividend income, safety of the original investment, and, if possible, capital appreciation. (See: *Speculator*)

Issue Any of a company's securities, or the act of disturbing such securities.

Legal List A list of investments selected by various states in which certain institutions and fiduciaries, such as insurance companies and banks, may invest. Legal lists are often restricted to high-quality securities meeting certain specifications. (See: *Prudent Man Rule*)

Leverage The effect on the per-share earnings of the common stock of a company when large sums must be paid for bond interest or preferred stock dividends, or both, before the common stock is entitled to share in earnings. Leverage may be advantageous for the common when earnings are good but may work against the common stock when earnings decline. Example: Company A has 1,000,000 shares of common stock outstanding, and no other securities. Earnings drop from $1,000,000 to $800,000 or from $1 to 80 cents a share, a decline of 20 percent. Company B also has 1,000,000 shares of common but must pay $500,000 annually in bond interest. If earnings amount to $1,000,000, there is $500,000 available for the common, or 50 cents a share. But earnings drop to $800,000, so there is only $300,000 available for the common, or 30 cents a share—a drop of 40 percent. Or suppose earnings of the company with only common stock increased from $1,000,000 to $1,500,000—earnings per share would go from $1 to $1.50, or an increase of 50 percent. But if earnings of the company which had to pay $500,000 in bond interest increased that much—earnings per common share would jump from 50 cents to $1 a share, or 100 percent. When a company has common stock only, no leverage exists because all earnings are available for the common, although relatively large fixed charges payable for lease of substantial plant assets may have an effect similar to that of a bond issue.

Liabilities All the claims against a corporation. Liabilities include accounts and wages and salaries payable, dividends declared payable, accrued taxes payable, fixed or long-term liabilities such as mortgage bonds, debentures, and bank loans. (See: *Assets, Balance Sheet*)

Lien A claim against property which has been pledged or mortgaged to secure the performance of an obligation. A bond is usually secured by a lien against specified property of a company. (See: *Bond*)

Liquidation The process of converting securities or other property into cash; the dissolution of a company, with cash remaining after sale of its assets and payment of all indebtedness being distributed to the shareholders.

Liquidity The ability of the market in a particular security to absorb a reasonable amount of buying or selling at reasonable price changes. Liquidity is one of the most important characteristics of a good market.

Listed Stock The stock of a company that is traded on a securities exchange, and for which a listing application and a registration statement, giving detailed information about the company and its operations, have been filed with the Securities & Exchange Commission, unless otherwise exempted, and the exchange itself. The various stock exchanges have different standards for listing. Some of the guides used by the New York Stock Exchange for an original listing are national interest in the company, a minimum of 1,000,000 shares outstanding with at least 800,000 shares publicly held among not less than 2,000 shareholders including at least 1,800 round-lot stockholders. The publicly held common shares should have a minimum aggregate market value of $14,000,000. The company should have net income in the latest year of over $2,-500,000 before Federal income tax and $2,000,000 in each of the preceding two years.

Load The portion of the offering price of shares of open-end investment companies which covers sales commissions and all other costs of distribution. The load is incurred only on purchase, there being, in most cases, no charge when the shares are sold (redeemed).

Locked In An investor is said to be locked in when he has a profit on a security he owns but does not sell because his profit would immediately become subject to the capital gains tax. (See: *Capital Gain or Capital Loss*)

Long Signifies ownership of securities: "I am long 100 U.S. Steel" means the speaker owns 100 shares. (See: *Short Position; Short Sale*)

Management The Board of Directors, elected by the stockholders, and the officers of the corporation, appointed by the Board of Directors.

Manipulation An illegal operation. Buying or selling a security for the purpose of creating false or misleading appearance of active trading or for the purpose of raising or depressing the price to induce purchase or sale by others.

Margin The amount paid by the customer when he uses his broker's credit to buy a security. Under Federal Reserve regulations, the initial margin required in the past 20 years has ranged from 40 percent of the purchase price all the way to 100 percent. (See: *Brokers' Loans; Equity; Margin Call*)

Margin Call A demand upon a customer to put up money or securities with the broker. The call is made when a purchase is made; also if a customer's equity in a margin account declines below a minimum standard set by the Exchange or by the firm. (See: *Margin*)

Market Price In the case of a security, market price is usually considered the last reported price at which the stock or bond sold.

Matched and Lost When two bids to buy the same stock are made on the trading floor simultaneously, and each bid is equal to or larger than the amount of stock offered, both bids are considered to be on an equal basis. So the two bidders flip a coin to decide who buys the stock. Also applies to offers to sell.

Maturity The date on which a loan or a bond or debenture comes due and is to be paid off.

Member Corporation A securities brokerage firm, organized as a corporation, with at least one member of the New York Stock Exchange who is a director and a holder of voting stock in the corporation. (See: *Member Firm*)

Member Firm A securities brokerage firm, organized as a corporation, with at least one member of the New York Stock Exchange, Inc., who is a director and a holder of voting stock in the corporation. (See: *Member Corporation*)

Member Organization This term includes New York Stock Exchange Member Firm *and* Member Corporation. The term participant when used with reference to a Member Organization includes general and limited partners of a Member Firm and holders of voting and non-voting stock in a Member corporation. (See: *Member Corporation; Member Firm*)

MIP Monthly Investment Plan. A pay-as-you-go method of buying New York Stock Exchange listed shares on a regular payment plan for as little as $40 a month, or $40 every three months.

Under MIP the investor buys stock by the dollars' worth—if the price advances, he gets fewer shares and if it declines, he gets more shares. He may discontinue purchases at any time without penalty. The commission ranges from 6 percent on small transactions to slightly below 1½ percent on larger transactions. (See: *Dollar Cost Averaging; Odd-Lot Dealer*)

Mortgage Bond A bond secured by a mortgage on a property. The value of the property may or may not equal the value of the so-called mortgage bonds issued against it. (See: *Bond; Debenture*)

Municipal Bond A bond issued by a state or a political subdivision, such as county, city, town, or village. The term also designates bonds issued by state agencies and authorities. In general, interest paid on municipal bonds is exempt from Federal income taxes.

Mutual Fund (See: *Investment Trust*)

NASD The National Association of Securities Dealers, Inc. An association of brokers and dealers in the over-the-counter securities business. The Association has the power to expel members who have been declared guilty of unethical practices. NASD is dedicated to—among other objectives—"adopt, administer and enforce rules of fair practice and rules to prevent fraudulent and manipulative acts and practices, and in general to promote just and equitable principles of trade for the protection of investors."

Negotiable Refers to a security the title to which is transferable by delivery. (See: *Good Delivery*)

Net Asset Value A term usually used in connection with investment trusts, meaning net asset value per share. It is common practice for an investment trust to compute its assets daily, or even twice daily, by totaling the market value of all securities owned. All liabilities are deducted, and the balance is divided by the number of shares outstanding. The resulting figure is the net asset value per share. (See: *Assets; Investment Trust*)

Net Change The change in the price of a security from the closing price on one day and the closing price on the following day on which the stock is traded. In the case of a stock which is entitled to a dividend one day, but is traded "ex-dividend" the next, the dividend is considered in computing the change. For example, if the closing market price of a stock on Monday—the last day it was entitled to receive a 50-cent dividend—was $45 a share, and $44.50 at the close of the next day, when it was "ex-dividend," the price would be considered unchanged. The same applies to a split-up of shares. A stock selling at $100 the day before a 2-for-1 split and trading the next day at $50 would be considered unchanged. If it sold at $51, it would be considered up $1. The net change is ordinarily the last figure in the stock price list. The mark +1⅛ means up $1.25 a share from the last sale on the previous day the stock traded. (See: *Ex-Dividend; Point; Split*)

New Issue A stock or bond sold by a corporation for the first time. Proceeds may be issued to retire outstanding securities of the company, for new plant or equipment, or for additional working capital.

Noncumulative A preferred stock on which unpaid dividends do not accrue. Omitted dividends are, as a rule, gone forever. (See: *Cumulative Preferred*)

NYSE Common Stock Index A composite index covering price movements of all common stocks listed on the "Big Board." It is based on the close of the market December 31, 1965, as 50.00 and is weighted according to the number of shares listed for each issue. The index is computed continuously by the Exchange's Market Data System and printed on the ticker tape each half hour. Point changes in the index are converted to dollars and cents so as to provide a meaningful measure of changes in the average price of listed stocks. The composite index is supplemented by separate indexes for four industry groups: industrials, transportation, utilities, and finances. (See: *Averages*)

Odd Lot An amount of stock less than the established 100-share unit or 10-share unit of trading: from 1 to 99 shares for the great majority of issues, 1 to 9 for so-called inactive stocks. (See: *Inactive Stock; Round Lot*)

Odd-Lot Dealer A member firm of the Exchange that buys and sells odd lots of stocks—1 to 9 shares in the case of stocks traded in 10-share units and 1 to 99 shares for 100-share units. The odd-lot dealer's customers are commission brokers acting on behalf of their customers. There are one or more odd-lot dealers who, under current practices, are ready to buy or sell, for their own accounts, odd lots in any stock at any time. Odd-lot prices are geared to the auction market. On an odd-lot market order, the odd-lot dealer's price is based on the first round-lot transaction which occurs on the floor following receipt at the trading post of the odd-lot order. The usual differential between the odd-lot price and the "effective" round-lot price is 12½ cents a share for stock selling below $55, 25 cents a share for stock at $55 or more. For example: You decide to buy 20 shares of ABC common at the market. Your order is transmitted by your commission broker to the representative of an odd-lot dealer at the post where ABC is traded. A few minutes later there is a 100-share transaction in ABC at $10 a share. The odd-lot price at which your order is immediately filled by the odd-lot dealer is $10.125 a share. If you had sold 20 shares of ABC, you would have received $9.875 a share. (See: *Commission Broker; Dealer; Inactive Stock; Round Lot; Transfer Tax*)

Off-Board This term may refer to transactions over-the-counter in unlisted securities, or to a transaction involving listed shares which was not executed on a national securities exchange. (See: *Over-the-Counter, Secondary Distribution*)

Offer The price at which a person is ready to sell. Opposed to bid, the price at which one is ready to buy. (See: *Bid and Asked*)

Open-End Investment Trust (See: *Investment Trust*)

Option A right to buy or sell specific securities or properties at a specified price within a specified time. (See: *Puts and Calls*)

Overbought An opinion as to price levels. May refer to a security which has had a sharp rise or to the market as a whole after a period of vigorous buying which, it may be argued, has left prices too high. (See: *Technical Position*)

Oversold An opinion—the reverse of overbought. A single security or a market which, it is believed, has declined to an unreasonable level. (See: *Technical Position*)

Over-The-Counter A market for securities made up of securities dealers who may or may not be members of a securities exchange. Over-the-counter is mainly a market made over the telephone. Thousands of companies have insufficient shares outstanding, stockholders, or earnings to warrant application for listing on the New York Stock Exchange, Inc. Securities of these companies are traded in the over-the-counter market between dealers who act either as principals or as brokers for customers. The over-the-counter market is the principal market for U.S. Government bonds and municipals and stocks of banks and insurance companies. (See: *NASD*)

Paper Profit An unrealized profit on a security still held. Paper profits become realized profits only when the security is sold.

Par In the case of a common share, par means a dollar amount assigned to the share by the company's charter. Par value may also be used to compute the dollar amount of the common shares on the balance sheet. Par value has little significance so far as market value of common stock is concerned. Many companies today issue no-par stock but give a stated per share value on the balance sheet. Par at one time was supposed to represent the value of the original investment behind each share in cash, goods, or services. In the case of preferred shares and bonds, however, par is important. It often signifies the dollar value upon which dividends on preferred stocks, and interest on bonds, are figured. The issuer of a 3 percent bond promises to pay that percentage of the bond's par value annually. (See: *Capitalization; Transfer Tax*)

Participating Preferred A preferred stock which is entitled to its stated dividend and, also, to additional dividends on a specified basis upon payment of dividends on the common stock.

Passed Dividend Omission of a regular or scheduled dividend.

Penny Stocks Low-priced issues, often highly speculative, selling at less than $1 a share. Frequently used as a term of disparagement, although a few penny stocks have developed into investment-caliber issues.

Point In the case of shares of stock, a point means $1. If General Motors shares rise 3 points, each share has risen $3. In the case of bonds a point means $10, since a bond is quoted as a percentage of $1,000. A bond that rises 3 points gains 3 percent of $1,000, or $30 in value. An advance from 87 to 90 would mean an advance in dollar value from $870 to $900 for each $1,000 bond. In the case of market averages, the word point means merely that and no more. If, for example, the Dow-Jones industrial average rises from 470.25 to 471.25, it has risen a point. A point in this average, however, is not equal to $1. (See: *Averages*)

Portfolio Holdings of securities by an individual or institution. A portfolio may contain bonds, preferred stocks, and common stocks of various types of enterprises.

Preferred Stock A class of stock with a claim on the company's earnings before payment may be made on the common stock and usually entitled to priority over common stock if company liquidates. Usually entitled to dividends at a specified rate—when declared by the Board of Directors and before payment of a dividend on the common stock—depending upon the terms of the issue. (See: *Cumulative Preferred*; *Participating Preferred*)

Premium The amount by which a preferred stock or bond may sell above its par value. In the case of a new issue of bonds or stocks, premium is the amount the market price rises over the original selling price. The term premium also refers to a charge sometimes made when a stock is borrowed to make delivery on a short sale. It may refer, also, to the redemption price of a bond or preferred stock if it is higher than face value. (See: *Corner; Short Sale*)

Price-Earnings Ratio The current market price of a share of stock divided by earnings per share for a twelve-month period. For example, a stock selling for $100 a share and earning $5 a share is said to be selling at a price-earnings ratio of 20 to 1.

Primary Distribution Also called primary offering. The original sale of a company's securities. (See: *Investment Banker; Secondary Distribution*)

Principal The person for whom a broker executes an order, or a dealer buying or selling for his own account. The term principal may also refer to a person's capital or to the face amount of a bond.

Proxy Written authorization given by a shareholder to someone else to represent him and vote his shares at a shareholders' meeting

Proxy Statement Information required by the SEG to be given stockholders as a prerequisite to solicitation of proxies for a security subject to the requirements of the Securities Exchange Act.

Prudent Man Rule An investment standard. In some states, the law requires that a fiduciary, such as a trustee, may invest the fund's money only in a list of securities designated by the state

—the so-called legal list. In other states, the trustee may invest in a security if it is one which a prudent man of discretion and intelligence, who is seeking a reasonable income and preservation of capital, would buy.

Puts and Calls Options which give the right to sell or buy a fixed amount of a certain stock at a specified price within a specified time. A put gives the holder the right to sell the stock; a call, the right to buy the stock. Puts are purchased by those who think a stock may go down. A put obligates the seller of the contract to take delivery of the stock and pay the specified price to the owner of the option within the time limit of the contract. The price specified in a put or call is usually close to the market price of the stock at the time the contract is made. Calls are purchased by those who think a stock may rise. A call gives the holder the right to buy the stock from the seller of the contract at the specified price within a fixed period of time. Put and call contracts are written for 30, 60, or 90 days, or longer. If the purchaser of a put or call does not wish to exercise the option, the price he paid for the option becomes a loss.

Quotation Often shortened to "quote." The highest bid to buy and the lowest offer to sell a security in a given market at a given time. If you ask your broker for a quote on a stock, he may answer something like "45¼ to 45½." This means that $45.25 is the highest price any buyer wanted to pay at the time the quote was given on the floor of the Exchange and that $45.50 was the lowest price which any seller would take at the same time. (See: *Bid and Asked*)

Rally A brisk rise following a decline in the general price level of the market, or of an individual stock.

Ratio of Collateral to Debt The number of times total stock margin debt is covered by total collateral value:

$$\frac{\text{Collateral Value}}{\text{Stock Margin Debt}} = \text{Ratio}$$

Realizing (See: *Profit Taking*)

Record Date The date on which you must be registered as a shareholder on the stock book of a company in order to receive a declared dividend or, among other things, to vote on company affairs. (See: *Ex-Dividend; Transfer*)

Redemption Price The price at which a bond may be redeemed before maturity, at the option of the issuing company. Redemption value also applies to the price the company must pay to call in certain types of preferred stock.

Refinancing Same as refunding. New securities are sold by a company, and the money is used to retire existing securities. The object may be to save interest costs, to extend the maturity of the loan, or both.

Registered Bond A bond that is registered on the books of the issuing company in the name of the owner. It can be transferred only when endorsed by the registered owner. (See: *Bearer Bond; Coupon Bond*)

Registered Representative Present name for the older term "customers' man." In a New York Stock Exchange Member Firm, a Registered Representative is a full-time employee who has met the requirements of the Exchange as to background and knowledge of the securities business. Also known as an Account Executive or Customer's Broker.

Registered Trader A member of the Exchange who trades in stocks on the Floor for an account in which he has an interest.

Registrar Usually a trust company or bank charged with the responsibility of preventing the issuance of more stock than authorized by a company. (See: *Transfer*)

Registration Before a public offering may be made of new securities by a company, or of outstanding securities by controlling stockholders—through the mails or in interstate commerce—the securities must be registered under the Securities Act of 1933. A registration statement is filed with the SEC by the issuer. It must disclose pertinent information relating to the company's operations, securities, and management, and the purpose of the public offering. Securities of railroads under jurisdiction of the Interstate Commerce Commission, and certain other types of securities, are exempted. On security offerings involving less than $300,000, less information is required.

Before a security may be admitted to dealings on a national securities exchange, it must be registered under the Securities Exchange Act of 1934. The application for registration must be filed with the exchange and the SEC by the company issuing the securities. It must disclose pertinent information relating to the company's operations, securities, and management. Registration may become effective 30 days after receipt by the SEC of the certification by the exchange of approval of listing and registration, or sooner by special order of the Commission.

Regulation T The Federal regulation governing the amount of credit that may be advanced by brokers and dealers to customers for the purchase of securities. (See: *Margin*)

Regulation U The Federal regulation governing the amount of credit that may be advanced by a bank to its customers for the purchase of listed stocks. (See: *Margin*)

Return (See: *Yield*)

Rights When a company wants to raise more funds by issuing additional securities, it may give its stockholders the opportunity, ahead of others, to buy the new securities in proportion to the number of shares each owns. The piece of paper evidencing this privilege is called a right. Because the additional stock is usually offered to stockholders below the current market price, rights ordinarily have a market value of their own and are actively traded. In most cases they must be exercised within a relatively short period. Failure to exercise or sell rights may result in actual loss to the holder. (See: *Warrant*)

Round Lot A unit of trading or a multiple thereof. On the NYSE the unit of trading is generally 100 shares in stocks and $1,000 par value in the case of bonds. In some inactive stocks, the unit of trading is 10 shares.

Seat A traditional figure of speech for a membership on an exchange. Price and admission requirements vary.

SEC The Securities and Exchange Commission, established by Congress to help protect investors. The SEC administers the Securities Act of 1933, the Securities Exchange Act of 1934, the Trust Indenture Act, the Investment Company Act, the Investment Advisers Act, and the Public Utility Holding Company Act.

Secondary Distribution Also known as a secondary offering. The redistribution of a block of stock some time after it has been sold by the issuing company. The sale is handled off the NYSE by a securities firm or group of firms, and the shares are usually offered at a fixed price that is related to the current market price of the stock. Usually the block is a large one, such as might be involved in the settlement of an estate. The security may be listed or unlisted. (See: *Exchange Distribution; Investment Banker; Primary Distribution; Special Offering; Syndicate*)

Seller's Option A special transaction on the NYSE that gives the seller the right to deliver the stock or bond at any time within a specified period, ranging from not less than six business days to not more than 60 days.

Serial Bond An issue which matures in relatively small amounts at periodic stated intervals.

Service Charge In April, 1970, an interim service charge was imposed on orders of 1,000 shares or less, pending establishment of a new commission rate schedule. The charge—not less than $15.00 or 50 percent of the minimum commission applicable to the order, whichever is less—was initially to remain in effect for 90 days.
In July, 1970, the service charge was extended for an indefinite period. It has been generally assumed that it will terminate with the adoption of a new commission schedule.

Short Covering Buying stock to return stock previously borrowed to make delivery on a short sale.

Short Position Stocks sold short and not covered as of a particular date. On the NYSE, a tabulation is issued once a month listing all issues on the Exchange in which there was a short position of 5,000 or more shares and issues in which the short position had changed by 2,000 or more shares in the preceding month. Short position also means the total amount of stock an individual has sold short and has not covered, as of a particular date. (See: *Margin; Short Sale; Up Tick*)

Short Sale A person who believes a stock will decline and sells it though he does not own any has made a short sale. For instance: You instruct your broker to sell short 100 shares of ABC. Your broker borrows the stock so he can deliver the 100 shares to the buyer. The money value of the shares borrowed is deposited by your broker with the lender. Sooner or later you must cover your short sale by buying the same amount of stock you borrowed for return to the lender. If you are able to buy ABC at a lower price than you sold it for, your profit is the difference between the two prices—not counting commissions and taxes. But if you have to pay more for the stock than the price you received, that is the amount of your loss. Stock exchange and Federal regulations govern and limit the conditions under which a short sale may be made on a national securities exchange. Sometimes a person will sell short a stock he already owns in order to protect a paper profit. This is known as selling short against the box. (See: *Margin; Premium; Up Tick*)

Sinking Fund Money regularly set aside by a company to redeem its bonds, debentures, or preferred stock from time to time as specified in the indenture or charter.

Special Bid A method of filling an order to buy a large block of stock on the floor of the New York Stock Exchange. In a special bid, the bidder for the block of stock—a pension fund, for instance—will pay a special commission to the broker who represents him in making the purchase. The seller does not pay a commission. The special bid is made on the floor of the Exchange at a fixed price, which may not be below the last sale of the security or the current bid in the regular market, whichever is higher. Member firms may sell this stock for customers directly to the buyer's broker during trading hours.

Special Offering Occasionally a large block of stock becomes available for sale that, because of its size and the market in that particular issue, calls for special handling. A notice is printed on the ticker tape announcing that the stock will be offered for sale on the NYSE floor at a fixed price. Member firms may buy this stock for customers directly from the seller's broker during trading hours. The price is usually based on the last transaction in the regular auction market. If there are more buyers than stock, allotments are made. Only the seller pays a commission on a special offering. (See: *Secondary Distribution*)

Specialist A member of the New York Stock Exchange who has two functions: First, to maintain an orderly market, insofar as reasonably practicable, in the stocks in which he is registered as a specialist. In order to maintain an orderly market, the Exchange expects the specialist to buy or sell for his own account, to a reasonable degree, when there is a temporary disparity between supply and demand. Second, the specialist acts as a broker's broker. When a commission broker on the Exchange floor receives a limit order, say, to buy at $50 a stock then selling at $60—he cannot wait at the post where the stock is traded until the price reaches the specified level. So he leaves the order with the specialist, who will try to execute it in the market if and when the stock declines to the specified price. At all times the specialist must put his customers' interests above his own. There are about 350 specialists on the NYSE. (See: *Book*)

Specialist Block Purchase Purchase by a specialist for his own account of a large block of stock outside the regular Exchange market. Such purchases may be made only when the sale of the block could not be made in the regular market within a reasonable time and at reasonable prices, and when the purchase by the specialist would aid him in maintaining a fair and orderly market. The specialist need not fill the orders on his book down to the purchase price.

Specialist Block Sale Opposite of the specialist block purchase. Under exceptional circumstances, the specialist may sell a block of stock outside the regular market on the Exchange for his own account at a price above the prevailing market. The price is negotiated between the specialist and the broker for the buyer. The specialist need not fill the orders on his book down to the purchase price.

Speculation The employment of funds by a speculator. Safety of principal is a secondary factor. (See: *Investment*)

Speculator One who is willing to assume a relatively large risk in the hope of gain. His principal concern is to increase his capital rather than his dividend income. The speculator may buy and sell the same day or speculate in an enterprise that he does not expect to be profitable for years. (See: *Investor*)

Split The division of the outstanding shares of a corporation into a larger number of shares. A 3-for-1 split by a company with 1,000,000 shares outstanding results in 3,000,000 shares outstanding. Each holder of 100 shares before the 3-for-1 split would have 300 shares, although his proportionate equity in the company would remain the same; 100 parts of 1,000,000 are the equivalent of 300 parts of 3,000,000. Ordinarily splits must be voted by directors and approved by shareholders. (See: *Stock Dividend*)

Stock Ahead Sometimes an investor who has entered an order to buy or sell a stock at a certain price will see transactions at that price reported on the ticker tape while his own order has not been executed. The reason is that other buy and sell orders at the same price came in to the specialist ahead of his and had priority. (See: *Book; Specialist*)

Stock Clearing Corporation A subsidiary of the New York Stock Exchange, Inc., which acts as a central agency for clearing firms in providing a "clearance operation" through which transactions made on the Floor are confirmed and balanced and, also, a "settlement operation," which handles the physical delivery of securities and money payments.

Stock Dividend A dividend paid in securities rather than cash. The dividend may be additional shares of the issuing company, or in shares of another company (usually a subsidiary) held by the company. (See: *Ex-Dividend; Split*)

Stockholder of Record A stockholder whose name is registered on the books of the issuing corporation. (See: *Ex-Dividend; Ex-Rights; Record Date*)

Stopped Stock A service performed—in most cases by the specialist—for an order given him by a commission broker. Let's say XYZ just sold at $50 a share. Broker A comes along with an order to buy 100 shares at the market. The lowest offer is $50.50. Broker A believes he can do better for his client than $50.50, perhaps might get the stock at $50.25. But he doesn't want to take a chance that he'll miss the market—that is, the next sale might be $50.50 and the following one even higher. So he asks the specialist if he will stop 100 at ½ ($50.50). The specialist agrees. The specialist guarantees Broker A he will get 100 shares at 50½ if the stock sells at that price. In the meantime, if the specialist or Broker A succeeds in executing the order at $50.25, the stop is called off. (See: *Specialist*)

Street The New York financial community in the Wall Street area.

Street Name Securities held in the name of a broker instead of his customer's name are said to be carried in street name. This occurs when the securities have been bought on margin or when the customer wishes the security to be held by the broker.

Switching Selling one security and buying another.

Syndicate A group of investment bankers who together underwrite and distribute a new issue of securities or a large block of an outstanding issue. (See: *Investment Banker*)

Tax-Exempt Bonds The securities of states, cities, and other public authorities specified under federal law, the interest on which is either wholly or partly exempt from Federal income taxes.

Technical Position A term applied to the various internal factors affecting the market; opposed to external forces such as earnings, dividends, political considerations, and general economic conditions. Some internal factors considered in appraising the market's technical position include the size of the short interest, whether the market has had a sustained advance or decline without interruption, a sharp advance or decline on small volume, and the amount of credit in use in the market. (See: *Overbought; Oversold*)

Thin Market A market in which there are comparatively few bids to buy or offers to sell or both. The phrase may apply to a single security or to the entire stock market. In a thin market, price fluctuations between transactions are usually larger than when the market is liquid. A thin market in a particular stock may reflect lack of interest in that issue or a limited supply of or demand for stock in the market. (See: *Bid and Asked; Liquidity; Offer*)

Ticker The instrument that prints prices and volume of security transactions in cities and towns throughout the U.S. and Canada within minutes after each trade on the floor.

Tips Supposedly "inside" information on corporation affairs.

Trader One who buys and sells for his own account for short-term profit. (See: *Investor; Speculator*)

Trading Floor (See: *Floor*)

Trading Post One of 18 horseshoe-shaped trading locations on the floor of the New York Stock Exchange at which stocks assigned to that location are bought and sold. About 75 stocks are traded at each post. (See: *Inactive Post*)

Transfer This term may refer to two different operations. For one, the delivery of a stock certificate from the seller's broker to the buyer's broker and legal change of ownership, normally accomplished within a few days. For another, the recording of the change of ownership on the books of the corporation by the transfer agent. When the purchaser's name is recorded on the books of the company, dividends, notices of meetings, proxies, financial reports, and all pertinent literature sent by the issuer to its securities holders are mailed direct to the new owner. (See: *Registrar; Street Name*)

Transfer Agent A transfer agent keeps a record of the name of each registered shareowner, his or her address, and the number of shares owned, and sees that certificates presented to his office for transfer are properly cancelled and new certificates issued in the name of the transferee. (See: *Registrar; Transfer*)

Transfer Tax A tax imposed by New York State when a security is sold or transferred from one person to another. The tax is paid by the seller. On sales by New York State residents, it ranges from 1.25 cents a share to 5 cents a share sold for $20 or more. Sales by out-of-state residents not employed in New York are taxed at reduced rates. There is no tax on transfers of bonds.

Treasury Stock Stock issued by a company but later reacquired. It may be held in the company's treasury indefinitely, reissued to the public, or retired. Treasury stock receives no dividends and has no vote while held by the company.

Turnover The volume of business in a security or the entire market. If turnover on the NYSE is reported at 10 million shares on a particular day, 10,000,000 shares changed hands. Odd-lot turnover is tabulated separately and ordinarily is not included in reported volume.

Two-Dollar Broker Members on the floor of the NYSE who execute orders for other brokers having more business at that time than they can handle themselves, or for firms who do not have their Exchange member-partner on the floor. The term derives from the time when these independent brokers received $2 per hundred shares for executing such orders. The fee is paid by the broker and today it varies with the price of the stock. (See *Commission Broker*)

Underwriter (See: *Investment Banker*)

Unlisted A security not listed on a stock exchange. (See *Over-the-Counter*)

Unlisted Trading Privileges On some exchanges a stock may be traded at the request of a member without any prior application by the company itself. The company has no agreement to conform with standards of the exchange. Today admission of a stock to unlisted trading privileges requires SEC approval of an application filed by the exchange. The information in the application must be made available by the exchange to the public. No unlisted stocks are traded on the New York Stock Exchange. (See: *Listed Stock*)

Up Tick A term used to designate a transaction made at a price higher than the preceding transaction. Also called a "plus-tick." A stock may be sold short only on an up tick, or on a "zero-plus" tick. A "zero-plus" tick is a term used for a transaction at the same price as the preceding trade but higher than the preceding different price.

Conversely, a down tick, or "minus tick," is a term used to designate a transaction made at a price lower than the preceding trade. A "zero-minus" tick is a transaction made at the same price as the preceding sale but lower than the preceding different price.

A plus sign, or a minus sign, is displayed throughout the day next to the last price of each company's stock traded at each trading post on the floor of the New York Stock Exchange. (See: *Short Sale*)

Voting Right The stockholder's right to vote his stock in the affairs of his company. Most common shares have one vote each. Preferred stock usually has the right to vote when preferred dividends are in default for a specified period. The right to vote may be delegated by the stockholder to another person. (See: *Cumulative Voting; Proxy*)

Warrant A certificate giving the holder the right to purchase securities at a stipulated price within a specified time limit or perpetually. Sometimes a warrant is offered with securities as an inducement to buy. (See: *Rights*)

When Issued A short form of "when, as and if issued." The term indicates a conditional transaction in a security authorized for issuance but not as yet actually issued. All "when issued" transactions are on an "if" basis, to be settled if and when the actual security is issued and the Exchange or National Association of Securities Dealers rules the transactions are to be settled.

Wire House A member firm of an exchange maintaining a communications network linking either its own branch offices, offices of correspondent firms, or a combination of such offices.

Working Control Theoretically, ownership of 51 percent of a company's voting stock is necessary to exercise control. In practice —and this is particularly true in the case of a large corporation— effective control sometimes can be exerted through ownership, individually or by a group acting in concert, of less than 50 percent.

Yield Also known as return. The dividends or interest paid by a company expressed as a percentage of the current price—or, if you own the security, of the price you originally paid. The return on a stock is figured by dividing the total of dividends paid in the preceding 12 months by the current market price—or, if you are the owner, the price you originally paid. A stock with a current market value of $40 a share which has paid $2 in dividends in the preceding 12 months is said to return 5 percent ($2.00 ÷ $40.00). If you paid $20 for the stock five years earlier, the stock would be returning you 10 percent on your original investment. The current return on a bond is figured the same way. A 3 percent $1,000 bond selling at $600 offers a return of 5 percent ($30 ÷ $600). Figuring the yield of a bond to maturity calls for a bond yield table. (See: *Dividend, Interest*)